The Love Clinic

the energy secrets of love, sex and relationships

Sandra Hillawi

Gosport, UK

9 Jan 2008

To Jan
with love

Sacha
x 🖤 x

The Love Clinic
The energy secrets of love, sex and relationships

© 2008

ISBN 10: 1873483201
ISBN 13: 978-1-873483-20-6
First Edition, First Printing

Published by
DragonRising Publishing
18 Marlow Avenue
Eastbourne
East Sussex BN22 8SJ
United Kingdom
www.DragonRising.com

Reviews

*S*andra Hillawi, a leading teacher of energy psychology, has written a wonderful book—a true inspirational manual on attracting, expressing, and nurturing love. With many clear illustrations, she describes in detail how to use EmoTrance, a remarkable and simple method of working directly and deeply with the felt energetics of emotions and thoughts. It is all too easy for human beings to become lost in concern with the content of our thoughts and feelings, failing to notice how these are expressed in our bodies and the energy field within and around us. Once we focus instead on these energetic aspects, the distress simply softens, melts, and flows away. Comparisons may be made with the popular mindfulness variants of contemporary cognitive therapy—but EmoTrance takes this many quantum steps further, resolving problems often in seconds that would take much longer using current conventional methods. Sandra's book is authentic, rooted in her own experiences and those of her clients. She tells of her journey, through EmoTrancing the obstacles deep in the energetics of her own beliefs and fears, to release her capacity to give and receive love—and to find her own soulmate. It is a lovely book, beautifully written from the heart. Sandra Hillawi 'walks her talk'—and her book is a gift.

Phil Mollon PhD, Clinical Psychologist and Psychoanalytic Energy Psychotherapist.
ACEP Consultant in Comprehensive Energy Psychology, Herts, UK

I am thrilled that Sandra Hillawi has taken it upon herself to make the latest research in energy work available to everyone. There is so much need for people to heal from their experiences with love, which have often been so much less than perfect. What is even more delightful is that Sandra shows us that what we have experienced in the past does not need to limit us for the future. I for one am extremely excited by the possibilities outlined in The Love Clinic, and have found Sandra's way of working with emotional pain to be logical, approachable and surprisingly easy. This is a book I would highly recommend to anyone who wants and needs more love in their life—and that would be the whole world.

Nicola Quinn, Reiki Master, UK

Buy this book. Feel the energy of the Sun flow through you. Let Sandra's clear instructions teach you how to learn to rest in the arms of the one that loves you best....You! I loved the bit about transforming tears, that's entirely new and such a relief! Such clarity of language, and deep understanding of the subject. Really really love it! A gorgeous and talented writer. No gimmicks, no hassle.....just resolution and well being...priceless....no, really, BUY THIS BOOK!

B.Salmon Hawk, MD Life Solutions, Herts, UK

What a book!! What a book!! What a book!! What a book!!

This book will show you how the human spirit is as magical and beautiful as a flower. Once you start practicing EmoTrance, You will touch your glowing beauty.. You will smell your growing charm ..You will see your bright magnificence..You will listen to your sacred music..You will walk your own heroic journey..all before your eyes..all before your eyes. I have to step back and bow and say God bless you Sandra...God bless you...

Dr E Sherif, Toronto, Canada

I loved this book! It arrived whilst I was still hurting from a recent break-up and was a God send. To people completely new to the concept of energy flow this book is so accessible. My ex had found someone else. The Love Clinic helped me release the hurt, anger and blame in my body and now I am only grateful, that he has released me from a destructive relationship that I would have found hard to leave and given me a golden opportunity to move forward in my life. I then used other chapters to attract a new man into my life. This is an absolute handbook for all stages of relationships. Thank you Sandra...for giving me the opportunity to remember IT'S ONLY ENERGY!!!

K.Oakley, Residential Care Worker, Shropshire, UK

What a great book. Even though we were on the original training together and that made an historic difference in both of our lives, I feel this book has much to offer both people new to personal development and existing practitioners alike with its wealth of experience since that time. I loved the simple and clear way you explain the whole energy concept and EmoTrance and generously offering various exercises giving opportunities for personal growth to all.

The personal success stories and exercises, makes a very important esoteric principle a very easy and fun read for all. I loved working with some of the exercises and am still glowing from the last one I did.

I love it, will read it again and expect to gain even more from it this time.

K.Baker, Reflexologist, Hants, UK

Sandra has put together a refreshingly simple guide making emotional freedom a genuine and achievable reality.

S.Bishop, Hypnotherapist, NLP Master, Berks, UK

Both gripping and enjoyable. Applying these concepts dramatically changed my life.

C.Brown, Driver, Fareham, UK

I enjoyed this book so much, once started is very hard to put down. Sandra's writing does keep you captivated.

C.Mansfield, Naturopath Middlesex, UK

John Lennon wrote 'Love is all you need'. Sandra so simply and easily shows how this can be achieved. Let the energy flow.

C. Davies, Retired Civil Servant, Hants, UK

Contents

About The Author

*S*andra Hillawi lives in Gosport Hampshire with a second home in Cairo follow-ing her recent marriage to her Egyptian husband Khaled. She is one of the UK's leading voices in the rapidly growing field of energy psychology following a number of years of private practice and teaching hundreds of workshops in the UK and inter-nationally. She started out with a BSc Hons Physics from Manchester University and a first career in Computing and made a radical change to Natural Healing following training as a Master Herbalist and Colonic Therapist in 1998. After her introduction to EFT in 2000 and EmoTrance in 2002 her subsequent interest in stress, the mind-body connection and emotional and spiritual health lead her from there to establish her career in energy psychology where she is now a recognised teacher and an engag-ing speaker in the field.

Acknowledgements

*F*irstly, I would like to acknowledge the Great Designer of this Creation, that created us as miraculous spiritual beings with the potential for great love and great joy when we follow the simple principles of the Even Flow.

Secondly, there are many pioneers in the field of energy psychology whose work has influenced me and helped to me to effect positive change within myself and subsequently with others. In particular I would like especially to acknowledge Dr Silvia Hartmann whose creative genius has been the inspiration and catalyst for much of my own personal growth and professional development over the last few years. Dr Hartmann's gift of EmoTrance for transforming emotional energy, understanding the human spirit and how we function in relation to the Creation that we are a part of has been the start of a great wave of healing, change and growth in consciousness of the energy dimension.

Thirdly, I would like to acknowledge my dear friends, colleagues and clients who contributed to this work by their personal experience and by their time in reviewing the manuscript of this my first book, Steve Bishop, Margarita Foley, Clare Brown, Kathie Oakley and not least my very dear friend Baya Salmon Hawk. Baya's facilitation, love and patience in helping me transform my own emotional energy over the last few years as my ET buddy, has helped me to heal, to overcome, to understand, to transform and has been an integral part of my personal and professional path, not to mention helping me overcome a year's procrastination about writing the book.

I want to thank my family for being who they are, for their support kindness despite how challenging my way of life is to them, and for challenging me to grow in patience, compassion and humility. And my dear Egyptian friends Esam Radwan and Mohamed Mahran who live and demonstrate human kindness and generosity of spirit far beyond any western ideas of love and friendship, and who have taught me so much about the possibilities and the greatness of the human heart.

Finally, I want to thank God for the beautiful spirit Mohamed Salama, also known as Khaled, who is my dear and beloved husband. Thank you Sweetheart for your unconditional acceptance, for knowing and understanding me, for your pure heart and, in spite of enormous challenges, for demonstrating your love and care for me in every aspect of your life in thought, word and deed. You have taught me so much and without you this book would not have come into existence. I love you and will love you till the end of my life.

This book is dedicated to you my Sweetheart.

Forward

By Dr Silvia Hartmann

What is YOUR experience of love?

Honestly, now

Are you disappointed?

Were you hurt?

Were you left confused, in pain, in turmoil by the power of love—or was there just never enough of it, or never the right kind, at the right time for you?

If any of that rings true to you, welcome to human race, my friend.

I've certainly had my share of love problems over the years.

On the one hand, you crave love like nothing else, and nothing else will do—we can eat and drink, we can sport and hobby, we can bury ourselves in work and keep ourselves occupied with rituals, repetitive tasks or poetry, for that matter—this is a hunger that never goes away.

Let's face it—we human beings were MADE FOR LOVE.

Then why is there that other hand?

That side of the coin where love hurts more than words can say, where loss of love brings you to your knees, where rejection, disinterest, random words spoken can rip your heart apart in an instant?

The truth is that we did not understand what love was.

We could feel it in our bodies, and we could feel the effects it had on our thoughts and how we would act, but no-one taught us how to do love right.

No-one knew!

But here's the good news.

We have had for the past five years a new definition of the workings of love—one that is simple, profound and actually true.

We know that it's true because it works.

It works for young children, middle aged academics, teenagers, and grand-mas; it works for soldiers, check out assistants and artists, and it even works for nuns. It works for Rabbis too—it has nothing to do with philosophy or with religion, there's nothing New Age about it—the new definition of love is simply the result of my life's work of observing how people really work, what really goes on with them, and then making a map of this which includes the energy system as a part of the body by definition.

We call this new map "EmoTrance", but that's not important here.

What *is* important is that we finally have a WORKING TOOL for our love problems.

Working with the energy system allows us—every single one of us!—to understand what's going wrong, and more importantly, have a way to fix it, so our love circuitry works as it was designed to work in the first place once more.

In this excellent book, First Generation EmoTrance Trainer Sandra Hillawi, who has worked with love and relationship problems as her speciality and who has helped so many people find a whole new delight in love and loving, giving and receiving this wonderful nourishment each one of us absolutely needs not just to survive, but to thrive in this world, explains to us in simple terms how we can use these new maps to literally transform our experiences of love.

Some of us may be immediately drawn to healing the old hurts and pains that still exist within us and that make every day a burden, rather than a wonderful new beginning.

Some of us may be drawn to the promise of reaching forward and making our existing relationships as deep, profound, beautiful and inspiring as we had always hoped that they might be.

Some of us may be hoping deep inside that the knowledge in this book will give us a chance to really find true love—just once, just for one moment, before we die—PLEASE!

For all of us who come with our own love problems and love questions, here is the Love Clinic. It is open and you can come inside, learn something new and be inspired by the examples from many people of all ages, all religions, from all around the world, who have found that this way of working can give them back control over their love life in a way they never dreamed.

Love isn't supposed to be difficult.

Love isn't meant to be hard.

Love was never designed to be painful.

Love is the most wonderful thing we can ever experience, giving and receiving, it makes life worth living, love IS what life is all about!

This book will let you in on the REAL energy secrets of love in all of its many splendoured ways and will give YOU what you need to make YOUR love life SPARKLE.

Wishing you joy beyond joy,
Dr Silvia Hartmann
Creator, EmoTrance
Author, *Oceans Of Energy*

Introduction

CHAPTER 1

The Problem With Love

*F*or most of us, relationships are not only the source of our deepest joy and happiness, but also our deepest stress and pain when they go wrong or they end. They start off well: we fall in love, life is wonderful, somebody loves us, and then things go wrong. Little hurts, lack of consideration, jealousy, insecurity, demands of work and pressures of life that cause us stress or take us away from our relationships, so we seek solace elsewhere when we don't get it at home. Or we actually dare to open up to someone and let them in, old wounds get triggered—the beloved is gone and a monster appears! We are faced with challenging behaviours that we don't know how to handle. We react in anger; words hurt. We close down and lose that loving feeling. Our relationships can go stale and behind those walls we are starving for love. We might fear opening up again. The phrase, "Once bitten twice shy" keeps us safe, but safe in what kind of existence? Life is ok, but it's not ecstatic—and yet it could be. And as for rapture, feeling that great? What is that? Is it beyond our experience? Yet, it could be your experience, very soon.

Apart from our romantic relationships there's family, friends, work and community life. Life happens, we get stressed, we speak and act from emotion, throw a tantrum. It's hard to handle for those around us; we lose our connection. Differences in lifestyle, sexuality, going through major life changes and transitions, changes at work, can all challenge our relationships leaving us feeling unsupported, unaccepted or misunderstood, vulnerable and unloved.

We all want more love in our lives. Let's face it—it is just the best feeling. We want to feel great, we want to feel loved. To truly love and be loved by another human being is one of life's most precious gifts. So why is it so elusive?

And if we were in love, how did we lose that love? If we haven't yet discovered love, why might that be? How can we attract or create more love in our life? And while we are asking, what exactly is love?

This book is about understanding negative and positive emotions. It's about understanding and transforming emotional energy. Transforming the pain, hurt, sadness, anger, fear, sadness, jealousy and neediness that gets in the way of joy, happiness, compassion and love. It's about being able to open up, feeling, letting people and life in, experiencing it fully and then letting it go. Really experiencing fully, and handling all that that entails beautifully, deeply, richly. It's about being in flow. It's about real deep nourishment of the heart and soul—whatever relationship we are in.

But before we can do all that, we need to understand more about our emotions, our energy system, the concept of flow, interruptions to flow and what we can do about that. A simple understanding and awareness can transform our lives and relationships creating all the love we desire. It's the simplest things that are the most profound. It's all about energy.

So herein lie...

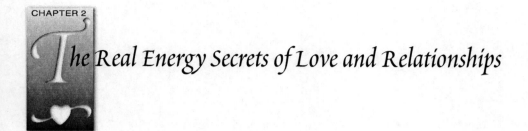

CHAPTER 2

The Real Energy Secrets of Love and Relationships

The secrets lie in the most simple, natural, elegant, profound and powerful system for transforming your emotional energy and restoring your natural state of being, which is love and joy.

This book will show you how. This book will not only show you, it will teach you and train you in the basic knowledge, understanding and awareness for feeling more love in your relationships with others, with yourself with your audience, with God—in fact with anything. From romantic love to spiritual love we will explore and release the problems which interrupt our flow. This book will train you in how to do this. It's a book for healing and transformation.

I was 38 when I found this knowledge, and started to apply the principles in this book. Until then I didn't know how to do that. This has been the single most important discovery in my life and has brought me the most important things in my life, and not just in my relationships. It has shown me how to transform my experience of life from the ordinary to the extraordinary, from just ok to deeply nourishing. It can do the same for you.

CHAPTER 3

Getting the Best From The Love Clinic

This book can be read from end to end or you can dip in and out at the chapters of interest. We start with the basics about energy, understanding emotions and how to transform emotional energy. Make sure you read the basics and do some of the practice exercises, which will help you to become fluent in the simple technique and at the same time you will explore how your energy system works and how you function as a person in relation to your environment. Doing the exercises will actually create real changes and transformation in you and your relationships. Start with basic practice exercises and progress through the exercises in the rest of the book, which explore different problems that arise in relationships in addition to attracting the relationship you want, and will help you to create the changes that you are seeking.

The book is designed for self-help, but also to encourage awareness among your circles of family, friends and colleagues so that you can assist each other along your personal development paths. Encouraging your friends to read this book is therefore a great idea. Some of the exercises are actually easier with a partner plus you can share with each other how things are changing for you as well as developing your own support network. After many years of working with these self help techniques I still work with my friends. There are still times when the energy of another person can not only make a huge difference, but also creates the opportunity for both the giving and receiving of healing and transformation, which is both a joyful and satisfying exchange and experience, enriching our friendships. There are also times when it is advisable to contact a qualified practitioner and this will be pointed out through the book as appropriate.

How the subtle energy system—our spirit person—interfaces with our physical body and brain creating the hormones that make our emotions or instructing the nervous system to contract or relax our muscles or to increase blood flow is not the subject of this book. Scientific understanding is growing and good books exploring the physics of healing and the biology of emotions and the mind-body connection are *The Field*[1] by Lynn McTaggart, *Molecules of Emotion*[2] by Candace Pert and *The Biology of Belief*[3] by Bruce Lipton.

I have included personal stories of my clients, my friends and myself through-out the book and many more in a separate section at the end. The stories give life to the concepts and principles at work and show how real people make real changes to create what they wanted following the transforming of their emotional energy. All the stories used in this book are true though all names have been changed to protect anonymity unless the source has specifically agreed to be named. I hope you find them inspiring and enlightening at the same time.

This book is about practical simple ways to create more love, happiness, and joy in your relationships, and in your life, working by yourself and working with a partner. Information about further resources available to you, such as qualified prac-titioners and workshops are at the back of the book. So let's begin.

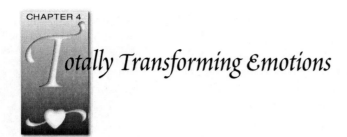

CHAPTER 4

*T*otally Transforming Emotions

*R*ecent developments in the field of energy psychology give us a new model for understanding emotions, where they come from, and how to deal with them. Our emotions arise as part of our human response to life experiences, but we now understand that emotions are a direct feedback response of the state of the body's subtle energy system.

We are spiritual beings. We have an energy system. As we respond to life, what people say and do to us, what happens, what we experience, all this is energy being processed in our energy body, by our spirit person. Just as our body has organs and channels for digesting the food we consume and extracting nourishment from it and releasing the wastes, our energy body or spirit person has energy centres and systems for handling the energies of life. Systems for deriving nourishment from those energies and for releasing what we don't need. Our experiences of those energies of life arise from the processing and flow of these energies in, through and out of our energy system. We don't just experience something in our brain, we also feel it in our body, like a kick in the stomach, a thump in the chest, a heaviness on the shoulders, or a thrill of excitement, a rush of warmth. These are real physical sensations. These emotions arise from states of flow or blockage in our system.

All of life is energy. All sights, sounds, fragrances, objects, what comes from people, words, songs, our environment, nature, the sun, stars, our own body—it's all energy. We are constantly interacting energetically with our environment.

Our energy body or spirit person is designed to handle, process and derive benefit from all of these natural energies.[4] As we take those energies in and experience them; when all is flowing in our energy system we get positive emotions: acceptance, understanding, enrichment, clarity, peace, happiness, compassion, joy, excitement, delight, rapture and love. This value and benefit that life energies bring us, we call energy nutrition.

When we don't handle life so gracefully, maybe because we have so much to handle or we are faced with a huge life event, such as a loss or trauma, these energies build up in our energy system causing a disturbance or blockage. Life continues to pour in, energy building upon more energy. This energy disturbance starts to hurt;

to cause us a pain in the chest, heaviness in the shoulders, tightness in the stomach or the head.

This energy build-up or disruption to healthy energy flow is now known to be **the actual cause** of our negative emotions.

All emotions, such as anger, guilt, pain, hurt, fear, shame, jealousy, anxiety, sadness, loss and worry, are accompanied by a physical sensation: pressure or pain in the chest, head, stomach, etc. This physical sensation is the location of the blocked energy. And while this energy is blocked, just like we have undigested food sitting in our system, which can disrupt the proper functioning of our physical body, so this energy blockage disrupts our spiritual functioning. We are emotional, we throw a fit, we blow a fuse, we are hurting. Meanwhile, just like our cells are not getting that nourishment because its still trapped in our digestive system, our spirit is not getting the full benefit of that particular life experience, the enrichment, the nourishment, the learning, the strengthening that is available when the energy of life can flow freely through and be released out.

CHAPTER 5

The Discovery of EmoTrance—How It All Began

*D*r Silvia Hartmann, a great pioneer and researcher in the field of personal development and energy healing in the UK, observed this phenomenon in 2002. She was chatting with her friend Nicola Quinn who was having an emotional rant about her boyfriend and complaining how much she was hurt by how he was treating her, and in particular, what he had said to her. It was actually hurting in her solar plexus, a real pain. Wanting to get past the winging to talk about something more interesting, Silvia asked, "Well, what can we do about this pain? Can we do something to release it? Where does it want to go?"

Nicola focussed on the pain and asked it, "Where do you want to go?" And the pain shot up, whooshed up and out of her head and she started laughing. It was gone. "Say those words to me again," she asked Silvia, to see if they would now hurt. The feeling again whooshed up and out of her head. The whole impact of what her boyfriend had said was gone, and she just laughed. They thought wow, that's interesting, and Silvia started to send more insults to Nicola. Noticing where the feeling came in, asking where it wants to go, the same thing happened. Then Nicola started to send insults to Silvia, but nothing happened. What they didn't know right then was that Silvia had strong barriers to that kind of comment. So instead, Nicola started to compliment her, called her a creative genius, and how wonderful she was.

"No, no; stop, stop," cried Silvia. "I can't take that, it hurts." Their experiments went on for an hour or so, paying attention to where that energy landed, softening the feeling and asking where does it want to go until they were so energised by all that they were doing and could handle all kinds of comments.

And so EmoTrance was born. The realisation that the negative emotion, anger, hurt and its accompanying physical pain was nothing more than an energy. By simply paying attention to that energy and where it was located in the body with the intention for it to soften and release, the energy flow was restored and with that flow, positive emotions were restored.

Other pioneers had discovered that energy disruptions in the body's subtle energy system were the cause of our negative emotions. Powerful transformation techniques such as TFT developed by Roger Callahan,[5] EFT by Gary Craig[6] and TAT by Tapas Flemming,[7] and many others, all work in various ways to release this energy and so create emotional freedom. They work by tapping or holding various energy release points, acupressure points, on the body, whilst tuned in to the distressing thought. Respected scholars and professionals such as Dr Phil Mollon[8] with courage, vision and dedication to education and healing have helped to bring these new tools into the more established psychoanalytic field through articles, books and training. Other great tools we have, such as NLP and Creative Visualistion all manipulate this energy at a higher level. All these are effective and powerful, but none were as simple, natural and easy as this.

With EmoTrance there are no tapping sequences, eye movements, steps to follow in a process, talking, revisiting old memories, clever visualisation or mental techniques. It is just simply to recognise that **what we feel** is energy, all energy and only energy and that the energy disturbance causing the emotional distress is located where the accompanying pressure or pain is, so we simply ask 'where do we feel that in our body?' We pay that energy some attention, and with the intention for it to soften, the energy starts to flow and to release. That is all that is required. This is the fundamental energetic level underlying all those other techniques. We were now working directly, purely and simply, with the body's energy system.

Little did Silvia and Nicola know of the magnitude and impact that their discovery would have and how this simple most natural process was going to transform the lives of thousands of people around the world. EmoTrance was launched in the UK at The Commonwealth Institute, Kensington, London in July 2002 by Silvia Hartmann. I was privileged to be among the intrigued, but sceptical audience at that launch event.

EmoTrance is simply shorthand for **Trans**forming **Emo**tional Energy. Why isn't called EmoTrans? No other reason than the domain name was already taken, so EmoTrance is what it became. It's nothing to do with hypnosis, or going into a trance, although it can create states of relaxation as we focus our attention and the energy gently releases.

With EmoTrance, when faced with an emotional problem we simply ask 'where do I/you feel this in my/your body?' and then we use our intention to soften the energy. As it softens it starts to spread and flow through the body. We have physical sensations such as warmth spreading, coolness flowing, tingling as the energy releases. Once the energy disturbance is released and energy flow restored we feel positive emotions, which arise from states of flow in the energy system.

It's a very simple and very natural process. You can do it for yourself. You can assist someone else to release some emotional energy with EmoTrance. You can use it in your professional practice, standalone or integrated into other therapies. You can use it at work; you can do it anywhere and with anyone, on a boat, plane, in a restaurant or at a party, (some of my best healing stories have come from these places!) as it's just like having a conversation with someone. People of all ages can benefit—even children, who can feel a pressure or pain in the body, but don't know how to verbally express their emotions. Releasing a problem with EmoTrance is content-free, which is also a blessing when releasing painful memories; we don't have to regurgitate all the details, cry buckets and need a whole box of Kleenex!

EmoTrance is about real healing that really works, based on actual reality. The person in pain knows when the problem has gone—they're not in pain anymore. What's more, that pain is replaced by a happier state and physical relaxation or even a thrill of excitement as a positive energy whooshes through their system. Silvia Hartmann's *Oceans of Energy*[4] is a great text book on the subject together with the sequel *Living Energy*.[9]

Once we start to apply EmoTrance for transforming emotional energy, we not only release the pain of negative emotions, but we start to experience and learn from real highs that life can give us. The energy of life and people can now flow freely and unobstructed through us, reconnecting us with the world. When we start living more fully, feeling even more alive, daring to really experience life—not just in our head but in our open heart, deep in our whole being—our experiences enrich our soul. As we open up and allow ourselves this nourishment of life and relationships we have more energy, and we become lighter and brighter; more 'attractive.' The Universal Law of Attraction[9] starts to work for us whenever we want. As bright spirits nourished and shining in our own right we are in a wonderful place to give and to share the best of ourselves with the world and the people around us.

We are now five years on and EmoTrance and its pioneers have matured in their understanding of our energy world through experience in the field and further research. Let's look now at the basic principles of transforming emotional energy, or EmoTrance.

EmoTrance – The Basics

1. In addition to our physical body, we have a spirit body or energy body, with an energy mind, heart, digestive system, elimination system, hands etc.

2. Our spirit body or person is designed to **handle, process and derive nourishment and benefit from all naturally occurring energies**: from people, nature, plants, music, the weather, etc.

3. There are no good or bad energies—just energy.

4. The experience of 'good' or 'bad' is down to how 'we' are handling that energy in our energy system at this moment.

5. Emotions are a direct feedback response of the state of the energy system—nothing more.

6. Negative emotions indicate blockage, injury, disturbance, deficiency.

7. Positive emotions indicate flow states.

8. We ask 'where do we feel this pain or injury, show me with your hands?'

9. We heal these energetic injuries by using our thought, or more precisely, intention.

10. We simply pay attention, say and think 'Soften and Flow' and the energy softens and releases through and out of the body.

11. We follow it until it's all released.

12. We test that it's all gone by returning to the original problem and repeating the process.

13. Having released the energy disturbance we have transformed the negative emotion and pain to a relaxation and calm or even fun and delight.

14. We call the natural state of our energy system 'The Even Flow,' resulting in positive states of happiness, joy, acceptance, thrills of delight, high energy, clarity, compassion and love—the natural states we are designed to experience.

CHAPTER 6

The Revelation: It's all Energy

One person can thrive under pressure; another can collapse under the very same pressure.

One person can be invigorated and energised by a rainstorm; another can shrivel up, close down and feel miserable in the same weather.

One person can cower and tremble in the face of confrontation; another can be relaxed, calm and resourceful.

One person can feel a rush and thrill receiving anger and criticism; another can curl up in pain in the corner at the same criticism.

One person can feel a warm glow of delight receiving a compliment or kindness; another can feel pain and tears letting it in.

One person has anxiety and fear in the face of adventure; another has only thrills and fun.

The incoming energy is the same, but the response—the way we handle it—is different.

Energy Needs to Flow

We are designed to handle all these different kinds of energies. When energy is flowing all is well. If we cannot handle a certain energy now, that's because energy flow is blocked, causing the negative emotional experience. We can learn how to simply and easily restore the flow in our energy system, thereby transforming the emotional energy from pain and blockage to flow and delight. Once the energy is released we feel energised, brighter and stronger; we laugh, we feel joy, fun and happiness. That's a healthy energy system.

In relationships, we have all kinds of energies to handle. So let's look at the different kinds of energies we get from people.

CHAPTER 7

Becoming Empowered by Criticism and Judgement

This is an energy that many find difficult to handle and we are faced with it in our daily lives from a very young age. We know the expression "sticks and stones may break my bones but names will never hurt me." Many of us know that to be false. Names do hurt us. We may not have a broken bone, but we absolutely feel that pain like a knife in the heart or a punch in the stomach. And that pain can endure through a lifetime. If we receive more insults and criticism, and feel more pain, we start putting up defences to keep these energies out, as it's far too painful to let them in. Then we become hardened and sometimes even aggressive to counter incoming energies. These shields and aggressive behaviour only indicate serious energetic injuries that are being protected.

But it doesn't have to be like that. We can let these energies in, find where it hurts, feel the injury in our energy system and heal that injury with our intention. We simply place our hands there, think soften and flow and feel where the energy wants to release.

"If you can bear to feel it, you can heal it"
                                                    ↷Janet Dedman

Not only can we restore the energy flow so criticism no longer hurts, but also we can learn to be energised and strengthened by this energy too. Try Exercise 1: Handling Criticism and Judgement (page 16), for some practice.

Handling Criticism and Judgement

Think of something that you know you would be offended or hurt by if someone said it to you. It might be about your physical appearance. When we were young, many of us had the pains of playground jibes or took to heart harsh words said to us. It may be about something you do or just something about you that you are sensitive about.

Here are a few ideas if you're stuck: you've put on weight; you're ugly; what have you done to your hair?; your ears really stick out; you'll never make it; you're a really bad person; you should say no more often; you're a doormat.

Send the trigger

Ask a friend to say that to you, or if you are doing this exercise alone, imagine someone is saying it to you. You may actually recall a specific event when someone did say that to you. You should feel an emotional response now.

Ask yourself: "Where do I feel this in my body?"

This is the location of the energy disturbance causing your emotional response. Notice what it feels like, how hard or soft it is.

Soften and flow

Place your hands there and think, it's only an energy; it's softening and flowing.

Hold your attention on the energy with the same thought (that it's softening) until you feel the energy start to flow.

Follow the energy on its path through your body until it finds an exit point.

Allow it all to release. If it slows down along the way and feels uncomfortable further along the path, again, just think "It's softening some more." Soft 'fluid' energy will find its way through and out of the body.

Test

Go back and test yourself again, get your friend to send you the criticism again, or imagine hearing it.

Repeat the process until there is no impact and until you feel the energy flowing smoothly in, through and out.

Notice how you feel now. It's the same energy, but now you're handling it better.

Get energised

Imagine you are receiving loads of insults, or get your friend to really hurl it at you. Take it all in, keep it softening and flowing through and out. Breathe into the flow. Notice how much stronger and energised you feel now. Appreciate that the insults and criticisms, which you thought were 'bad energies,' are now making you feel great.

There is no good or bad energy, only energy. All energies have some benefit for us. This is what we mean by 'energy nutrition.'

Questions

I can handle the energy, and now it doesn't hurt me any more, but I feel nothing.

Sometimes, when we are more resourceful, because we are no longer hurting, we choose to deflect the energy, and not to allow it in. That's one result and may be enough for one person. But we can go further. Try being consciously open and really allowing yourself to feel it again. Really open yourself and allow the comments in, feel them. Soften and flow the injuries until all the energy is flowing and you feel until you feel a more energised state.

I can't feel anything. I'm numb.

What you are experiencing are your shields, which are holding the energy back, outside of your body, to protect you. Put your sensors out to 'feel' how it feels outside your body. Ask, how close can those comments come. Where do they stop? This is where your shield is located. How to identify and deal with shields in a safe and comfortable way is covered later in this book.

I feel great, but will it last?

If you got energised, chances are it will. If you find sensitivity returning just notice if it's actually a different kind of comment or energy. You can learn to handle this in the same way. The more you handle, the more flow in your system, the easier it gets, and you start to make permanent changes.

Also bear in mind that we are creating flow in a channel into and through which life continues to happen. We need to keep processing and releasing to keep ourselves in flow. When we build up a strong flow, we develop a capacity to handle more of life. However, it doesn't mean that a huge event, or having many different things going on at once cannot dam up the channel again causing you to feel stressed or down. But now we understand that it's simply an energy build-up and blockage, and we can restore the flow again.

I can't get the energy to soften.

This may be because you are trying too hard to soften it, somehow using your willpower as opposed to your intention. There's a subtle difference with dramatically different effects. Intention is simply to 'think that something is happening', to think of 'the result you want.' Energy responds instantly and immediately to intention. Take a relaxed breath, observe what the energy feels like and just watch it. While watching it, think of it softening and flowing. That should do it.

It still won't soften.

Then there may be other psychological reasons for not letting go of this, which are coming from other energy disturbances, maybe in the same place, or maybe elsewhere in the body. We can either soften and release these first and then go back to the other disturbance and see how easily it now releases.

CHAPTER 8

Blossoming With Compliments and Appreciation

Many people find this even harder to do than the first exercise. When someone pays you a compliment do you blush with embarrassment? Do you deflect it and shake it off because you're uncomfortable? You don't believe they are sincere? Or maybe they want something from you? Does it prompt tears as it actually hurts you in the heart? Do you feel anything at all? Some of us never learned how to handle praise because we never received it when we were younger, so never got the practice. Some of us got it, but it came with strings attached, so we became guarded. And of course, some of us did get some practice growing up handling this kind of energy, and those people tend to be the ones coming into adulthood with a high self esteem, and are open and able to handle life more resourcefully. But even those who think they can receive it can probably get even deeper nourishment than what they are feeling now. So before we start blaming our parents for what they did and didn't do, in general they did their best with the resources they had. We can start from now to make up for what we didn't have and make positive changes for ourselves.

This kind of energy is designed to make you feel great, to feel warm, energised, and make you feel really good about yourself—if we can allow it in and handle it well. It's what we are seeking and hoping for in our work, play, sports and relationships.

Use Exercise 2: Handling Compliments, Praise and Appreciation, and then compare how you feel transforming this kind of energy in, through and out. How much better do you feel? How does it compare to getting energised from insults and criticism?

Handling Compliments, Praise
and Appreciation

Think of something that you would like to hear someone say to you, that you would like to believe about yourself, qualities that perhaps you don't quite believe that you have, or something that you would like someone to recognise about you.

Again, if you are stuck for ideas here's a few suggestions : you're beautiful; you are so kind; you're a really lovable person; you're so intelligent; you're really attractive; you're a great mother/father/teacher/healer/leader.

Send the Trigger

Ask a friend to say that to you, or if you are doing this exercise alone, imagine someone is saying it to you. You should feel an emotional response.

Ask yourself 'where do I feel this in my body?'

This is the location of the energy disturbance causing your emotional response. Notice what it feels like, how hard or soft. Maybe it feels good, but the energy is located just in your head or just in your chest.

Soften and Flow

Place your hands there and think, it's only an energy; it's softening and flowing.

Hold your attention on the energy with the same thought, that 'it's softening,' until you feel the energy start to flow.

Follow the energy on its path through your body until it finds an exit point.

Allow it all to release.

Test

Go back and test yourself again, get your friend to say the comment again, or imagine hearing it.

Repeat the process until there is no impact and until you feel the energy flowing smoothly in, through and out.

Notice how you feel now. It's the same energy, but now you're handling it better.

Get Energised

Imagine you are receiving loads of compliments and praise. Get your friend to really shower you with recognition and praise. Take it all in, keep it softening and flowing through and out. Breathe into the flow. Notice how much stronger and energised you feel now. Appreciate that these comments are also energies. Compare this energised state to the Energised state of the Criticism Exercise.

Exercise continued on next page

There is no good or bad energy, only energy. All energies have some benefit for us. This is what we mean by 'energy nutrition.' Notice just how much more nourishing this kind of energy is. Being able to really receive this kind of energy nutrition is transformational in building confidence and self esteem.

Think about what that means to you. Think about what that could mean to those around you, who are also thirsty for this kind of recognition, if you took more time to pay them that attention and to appreciate them more.

Questions

I can't feel anything. I'm numb.

What you are experiencing are your shields, which are holding the energy back, outside of your body, to protect you. Put your sensors out to 'feel' how it feels outside your body. Ask, 'How close can those comments come. Where do they stop?' This is where your shield is located. How to identify and deal with shields in a safe and comfortable way is covered in the appropriate chapter.

But why do I have to let go of this good feeling in my heart?

If the 'feeling' is localised then by definition the energy is not flowing throughout your system, and there are parts of you not receiving this nourishment. When you allow it to soften and flow, much more of you gets to feel good. You feel good all over! You received the energy nutrition from this. The chances are you not only have learned to handle this kind of energy now, but being this well nourished you don't 'need' this kind of energy so much anymore. Then when we look at how the Law of Attraction works, once you already feel this way about yourself, you will attract a lot more of this in your life! While we are still holding on to even a 'good' feeling in one part of our body, we are creating an obstruction to the flow of universal energy. You cannot attract that energy. The consequential deficiency elsewhere in your energy system may be giving rise to behaviours in you where you seek out this kind of energy in your relationships or life, as opposed to just allowing it to come.

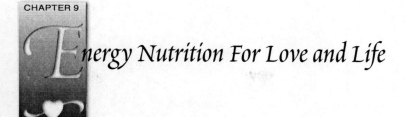

CHAPTER 9

Energy Nutrition For Love and Life

*E*very one needs a constant variety of energy nutrients flowing through their system for health and wellbeing. The nourishment we can get from people and from our relationships is very important for our health and happiness. In Exercise 2: Handling Compliments, Praise and Appreciation, most people find it feels so much better; they feel so much more nourished when they can accept appreciation from another person.

So we learn that different energies have different nutrients or benefits to bring. Just like the food we eat has different nutritional elements within, some more powerfully nourishing and helpful, some less so, from broccoli to cucumber, from blueberries to honeydew melon. We need a wide variety of energy nutrients for the health of the spirit, our emotional wellbeing, just as our physical body needs a wide variety of physical nutrients for its healthy functioning.

Feasting on Wonderful Energies

We are surrounded by oceans of energy, from the weather, nature, music, food, people, colours, objects, our work, etc. We can derive deeper nourishment from all of these energies and thus have a deeper and richer relationship with our environment and Creation of which we are a part.

Try inviting in other kinds of energies with Exercise 3: Other Kinds of Energy Nutrition (page 22).

Comments About Other Kinds of Energy Nutrition

"I was walking past a fish and chip shop and got the wonderful smell of English fish, chips and vinegar and an instant desire to go and get some. Instead I noted the sensations in my body, and then I softened and flowed them through and out. It felt fantastic that I'd got the satisfied feeling of having enjoyed the fish and chips, without actually spending or consuming unnecessary calories and living with the after effects. Very cool."

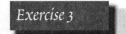

Other Kinds of Energy Nutrition

The Sun

Try taking in the energy of the sun; really feel its warmth and power on your skin. Have the intention to absorb it. Think 'soften and flow' and let that energy flow through all of your body, nourishing you deeply. Try it with a landscape, or a sunset, or a sea scape, a tree or flower. Invite the energy in, soften and flow, and release it. Explore how energising it can be.

Music

Explore and experience music on a deeper level. Listen and note how you feel. Soften and flow the sensations and allow the energy to flow through you. Try it with music you like, and with music you don't like. What changes?

Colours

Again, notice what colours you like and which ones grate on you. Can you soften and flow the energy of that grating feeling? How does that colour feel afterwards? What did you get from that?

Food

This is a great exercise for our cravings. Think of what you want, even see what you desire. Feel 'where is that in my body?' Soften and flow. Invite the energy of that food in through and out, and notice how that feels. Note what has happened to the craving now. How satisfied are you by the energy? Try it with other cravings.

Shopping, Cars, People

Do the same for those buying impulses; the car we fancy; the people we like; the qualities we would like for ourselves.

Here's a good one, try handling the energy of an audience that you are standing in front of. So many people struggle with that! I can personally vouch for the fact that this can be a thrilling, invigorating, enriching and wonderful experience. For many, that might need a little more work though, but you can get there. There is more on the subject of Love and Your Audience and Performance later in the book.

Explore, play, learn and navigate the oceans of energy around you. There is so much more fun, thrills and joy we can have engaging more deeply with the world about us. Use these exercises for practice, awareness, understanding, enrichment and joy.

"I was driving home from a course in Edinburgh and decided to take in the energy of Edinburgh Castle. Wow, what a hit! It was amazing energy through my body."

"I was in New York for the first time, and I noticed the strong energy of the city coming from the tall buildings and long straight streets of Manhattan, channelling the city's energy. I took it in and it was so invigorating and energising. I just love New York energy."

"I tried listening to some music that I liked, but this time with EmoTrance. I invited in the energy, softened and flowed it, and wow, this was an experience of music on a whole new level. Fantastic!"

See also "Ecstasy and Oneness on the Subway" on page 175.

$\mathcal{M}$astering Your Thoughts

$\mathcal{N}$ow we know how to transform different kinds of energies that we have to deal with in our relationships; transforming pain to joy and delight.

As a human being, a spirit person, we are handling all kinds of life events all the time. Either:

ᴄᴀ We handle them gracefully, in which case we ingest it, digest it and eliminate it, learning and growing in the process. In this case recalling the memory is a peaceful and enriching moment; OR

ᴄᴀ We still have energy indigestion and recalling that memory makes us feel pain, discomfort and distress, arising from the energy disturbance.

The same transformation of energy can be applied to the disturbances causing our distressing thoughts. When we think about a person, or something that they did, or something that happened, we feel the emotion and we ask, 'where do I feel that in my body?' Then we follow the same process of thinking 'soften and flow' until it all releases. Then we test, going back to the original thought and noting how it now feels. What's remaining? And we release the remaining energy in the same way until we have totally restored the Even Flow in our energy body. Then we can think of what happened, and we feel clarity, peace or energised and happy, and we have learned whatever that event had to teach us or bring us.

Learn to release these negative energies with Exercise 4: Releasing a Distressing Memory or Thought.

Releasing a Distressing
Memory or Thought

For your practice exercise don't choose a major life problem! You can deal with these later when you have more skill and understanding or with an EmoTrance Practitioner or with an EmoTrance (ET) friend who has had some working knowledge of transforming energy, either through this book or at a workshop.

So choose something medium sized for this exercise; for example, something that happened that you are still bothered about. It may be recent or it may be older. Or something that is going on at work or in the family that's worrying you.

Tune In

When you tune into this memory or thought, ask 'where do I feel this in my body?'

If you are working with a partner, they can ask you to think about it, and then ask you 'where do you feel it in your body?'

Use Your Hands

Place your hands hovering on your body in this area. You don't have to do this, but it helps a bit extra.

Think **'It's all energy, only energy, and its softening and flowing.'**

Let it Release

Allow the energy to find a release path through the body until it exits. Keep your attention with the energy, thinking 'soften and flow' until it has all released.

Test

Return to the memory and check how it feels now. If there is any remaining disturbance, repeat until you feel relaxed.

Get Energised

You can take this to the next step if you like. By visualising what happened even more strongly, get a friend to help you be creative here. This is a stronger energy to handle and therefore will give you a more energising experience when you can handle it.

Practice with other distressing memories.

CHAPTER 11

Do I Need Help?

Once you have had some practice releasing smaller and medium intensity memories, you may wish to tackle something a bit bigger or a bit more complex. The same principles apply. Deeper and more complex problems will benefit from the added energy of another person.

An EmoTrance Practitioner is a person who has the basic understanding and skills of transforming emotional energy and who has started to develop themselves by transforming their own emotional energy. They 'walk the talk' which means they 'live energy flow principles' in their daily lives already. This means they will also have developed their own energy system to be able to handle whatever you may have to revisit. For you, this means you will have a space of openness and acceptance and love—a safe space in which to work through releasing your own energies, which may be old and sometimes painful until you start to release them.

EmoTrance Practitioners don't wear white coats, uniforms or work from a place of distance or authority. They are just another human being who has learned how to help another human being to repair the injuries in their spirit/energy body back to the Even Flow. Two people working together with the best intention to restore the Even Flow. Anyone can lean learn to become an EmoTrance practitioner.

Even if problems are not major, but there is just a lot of it to release—many different memories and events that you are still holding onto—working with another person can help you release energy more quickly. Their energy and intention adds to your intention to make the process more effective, plus their open flowing energy system offering you that acceptance is a channel in itself for your energy to release through.

For a list of EmoTrance Practitioners and a list of international training workshops, visit the Additional Resources section. I recommend that you experience, at least once, working with an EmoTrance practitioner.

CHAPTER 12

Concepts of Love

A concept is a more complex energetic entity composed of our experience, our learning, emotions, feelings and beliefs. What we believe determines the way our life works. Using a global concept and working with the energy of that concept can be a way of changing how things work for you in your life, without going into all the details of how you came to think and believe what you believe and how you came to feel what you feel. We just work with the energy of the concept, change the energetics and watch how our life changes.

For example, the concept of 'a romantic relationship' contains a lot of information from different sources and experiences. It's a complex energetic entity in its own right. Your relationship with this concept determines how romantic relationships are operating in your life and what your actual experience is.

So again, as in the last section, we will be transforming the energy we are working with. But this time we are using a thought; i.e. an internal trigger for an energy disturbance, as opposed to handling an incoming energy from a person or the environment. This way we think of the subject, the concept, and then ask, 'where do we feel that?'

The Career Woman

This is a personal story. For many years I didn't have a long-term relationship. I explored this with an ET friend, Steve. We explored where the energy of this concept resided. He asked me, "When you think about the concept of relationships, where does that live?" No surprise that I felt nothing in my body about that. I scanned around outside my body sensing the space around me near to my body and far from my body. That was interesting; I had a sense of it being "over there." I pointed to what felt like a dense dark energy up and to the right, and in the distance.

Out of interest Steve asked, "Think about the concept of work and tell me what it feels like; where this energy is." I had a great feeling of flow, in, through and around me. It felt good and invigorating. In actual fact, work was going well, my business was thriving and I was happy in it. We discussed that maybe if the energy of my concept of relationships was flowing better that might allow me to attract one into my life!

Energy Needs to Flow In, Through and Out

So as "energy needs to flow, in, through and out," Steve directed me to put my attention on the relationships energy out there; to think of it softening and to invite it towards me, in, through and out. There was some resistance in my body, which I had to soften and flow, but eventually I got it all flowing through me in a strong energising way. It felt very different. Next we needed to think of both concepts together, relationships AND work to see if there was any conflict. There was. It was a pressure in the chest. We softened and restored the flow until both energies simultaneously were flowing well. That was in May 2005. The next month circumstances arose, which led to me meeting the man who, after a very short time, I just knew was the one for me. There is a little more to the story of what other changes I had made in myself leading up to that, but I will share that later.

You can use this process to change the energetics and therefore your actual experience in life of many different concepts that you have. Exercise 5: Changing Your Concepts in Relationships, suggests what you might choose and how to do that. Explore and observe how things change in your life when the energy flow changes.

Changing Your Concepts in Relationships

Work with a concept that's relevant to you, where you know you would like to change something about that in your life and relationships. Here are some ideas. You may have other ideas.

Relationships	Soul Mate	Passion
Rejection	Commitment	Money
Trust	Intimacy	Sex
Orgasm	Love	Marriage
Family	Men	Women
Homosexual	Gay	Lesbian
Childbirth	Teenagers	Responsibility
Religion	Politics	Business

As you tune into your chosen concept, think 'where do I feel this?' It may be inside your body. If you don't feel anything, scan outside your body by sensing what it feels like out there. Maybe you have a disturbance in your wider energy field. Maybe you have multiple energy disturbances around that concept, as it is a complex thing. Soften and flow the energy inside your body first. Then go to any energy outside, put your attention there, soften the energy and invite it towards you. As it flows in, check if you start to feel any further discomfort. If you do, then clear that first, then continue to bring the energy in, through and out, until it's all flowing freely.

Tune back into the concept again and see what's changed. How is your thinking different? How different does that feel now? Are there any new energy disturbances to clear? Repeat until you feel clear and energised and then just observe how things change in your life in relation to this concept now that the energetics have changed.

The Love Clinic in Practice

CHAPTER 13

The Love Clinic in Practice

So now we have some basic understanding of energy—that emotions are nothing more than a symptom; a feedback device indicating the health and state of our energy system. This is great news, as we don't have to beat ourselves up anymore because we are feeling sad, or because we get angry. We can do something about that—transform that energy.

Difficult emotions such as anger, fear, hurt, sadness, anxiety, loss, shame, jealousy and rage arise from energy build up, pressure, disturbance, blockage or deficiency in the energy system, which is our spirit person. In the same way that we may get indigestion, constipation pain, or nutritional deficiency diseases in our physical body, we can have the energetic analogy in our energy body.

Inability to take in and really digest and understand is 'energy indigestion.' The inability to let go emotionally is a kind of 'energy constipation!' As these situations persist chronically, we become energy deficient, which then leads us to behaviours that try to address those deficiencies, or to avoidance behaviours of the physical discomfort and pain caused by stuck energy.

So we need to feel where the disturbance resides, and then use our intention to soften and flow, allowing the pressure to release. Restoring the Even Flow of health in the energy system gives rise to positive emotional states of happiness, joy, peace, compassion, thrills, delight, rapture and love, with love being ultimate flow. This leads us to new insights and understandings about love.

If we feel anger and speak and act in anger, then what comes first, what is behind this anger, is the state of pressure or blockage in the energy system. Even if a person doesn't speak, we can 'feel' or sense that anger, because we are picking up the energy.

In the same way, if we feel love, and speak and act in love, what is behind this is the state of flow in the energy system. As love flows within us we radiate love. We will learn and explore more about this in future chapters, exercises and in the real love stories illustrating this later in this book.

We also know that energy needs to flow for healthy functioning and that when it flows we get nourished and derive some benefit, learning or enrichment in some way. And that Energy Nutrition is as essential to our health as the physical nutrients on our plate, which get digested, absorbed, transported and metabolised, regenerating us. The by products are transported and eliminated in a healthy flowing system. On a physical level we are what we eat. On a spiritual level we are what we experience, fully, in, through and out.

When we have indigestion, physically or energetically, we don't get the benefit yet of that physical or spiritual food.

Energy Outside the Body

I shared an example earlier of an energy disturbance residing in the wider energy field, outside the physical body. Our energy system does in fact extend beyond the skin barrier, but how far? This is an interesting question. We have the concept of our aura, but we also have the concept that we are all one energetic organism, one being. We can often sense these disturbances as 'something out there,' 'behind us,' 'on our shoulder,' 'around us,' 'a pressure bearing down.' In fact, a number of people with 'depression' I have worked with described it exactly as that—a sense of pressure bearing down, in addition to physical pressures within. The reason the disturbance is outside is often because it's more comfortable outside for us right now. In other words, to allow it in would be too painful and uncomfortable, or we simply cannot handle it. We are at our limit of what we can handle. But all energy needs to flow in, through and out for us to receive the learning or benefit it holds for us. So we simply notice where it is, have the intention for it to soften, and when it's soft enough, we invite it in, allow it to flow through and out, softening and releasing any injuries it triggers along its path. And if the pathway for it to flow into us is so blocked, then first we need to release the energetic plugs, open up those release valves and simply allow some of that pressure to release. After that we are able to process what's hanging around in our wider field. The energy world view can totally simplify our understanding of our complex emotional problems.

So now we are ready to apply these basic principles and techniques to the whole range of challenges and problems in our relationships to help us experience more flow states and ultimately more love in all aspects of our life.

After all, isn't that what we all want, and what we are here for?

CHAPTER 14

Overcoming Old Love Trauma

What happened to us in our past relationships and experience can and will have an impact on our current relationships—especially if we didn't process and release it fully.

An old painful memory or series of painful memories exist in our energy body as a series of old blockages, disrupting the flow of energy. These get triggered with new experiences in our current relationship. The new energy comes in, attempting to flow through, and hits an obstacle in its path—just as the water of a brook will be stopped in its tracks when it reaches the site of a landslide or a large boulder in its path. All the land down stream is dry and barren. The incoming energy triggers the negative emotional response from the energy block in its path. The energy block can build up with new experiences piling one on top of the other in the same place, making this like a dense hard energy in this part of the energy body. Initially we may only feel this on occasions when it gets triggered by a certain kind of experience. Eventually it can become persistent that we feel it all the time: 'the brick' in the solar plexus when all tests show us there's nothing physically wrong with us, and the chronic behaviour patterns coming from it.

All life experiences are energetic. Different past energetic events or experiences may be stored in different places, so recalling different memories may bring pains up in different parts of the body. Some may feel them all in the same place.

Is it fair to our new partner that the behaviour we show them in response to what they say and do for us, is actually the result of the pains of the past? Especially now, when we have the knowledge and tools to do something about that and become closer to the best we can be, which will benefit our partner more.

It's interesting also, the way life sends to us, or the way we attract, certain kinds of experiences, to teach us something. Until we have processed it properly, life has a funny way of sending the same kind of experience to us, knocking louder and louder at that door, until we actually decide to deal with it properly, to embrace it fully, digest it, assimilate it AND let it go. Once we have done that and have flow then we've had the learning and transformation; i.e. the energy nutrition. From there we can move on and attract a different kind of experience.

Why Do I Always Attract A Certain Kind of Person?

A client asked me this week, "Why do I always attract men who make me feel small?"

She had a sense that it came from her childhood. Her father always made her feel so small. Then in her adult life she attracted men who made her feel the same. Each new experience condensed or consolidated the previous ones, leading to a belief that she doesn't even deserve a good man. This was a solid rock feeling in her solar plexus. It is not surprising that she has digestive problems with food too. Although that's not the focus of this book I wouldn't be surprised at all to learn that everything relaxes physically once all of this hard energy is released.

In order to change what she is attracting she needs to repair her energy system.

When she has restored the flow of those original and successive events, which is still stuck in her energetic digestive system, she will then gain the real nourishment, growth and learning available from those experiences.

Her flow has been restored and she will now experience a very different pattern in men that she will attract from now on.

When we have past energetic injuries or painful memories, it actually hurts us when we open up to another person and let their energy in, so we become more guarded about being open. We only let someone in a bit at a time, until we are sure it's safe to be completely open. This can lead to fear of intimacy and is likely to be a relationship that is less connected, joyful and loving than it could be.

A partner may even become impatient that they are not fully accepted. They can't get through to the person and find that is a problem for them too.

So being able to release past painful memories and repair these old energetic injuries is good for us and it's good for our relationship. We will feel stronger, more open, confident and positive. The energy of flow within us is stronger and more attractive than the closed guarded protected energy. We radiate more. The more you let another person in, the deeper the joy and the deeper the love and connection that is available to you.

Use Exercise 6: Letting Go of the Painful Past, to release past painful memories. You can do this alone or for bigger, more complex memories, I highly recommend the help of an EmoTrance Practitioner or an experienced ET friend.

Create Your Own Support Network

Over the years I have developed a network of friends and colleagues who all understand and use these principles in their lives. We are a great support to each other. By introducing your friends to these concepts they can start to learn and apply these

Letting Go of the Painful Past

You may have had several past painful relationships. So let's approach this systematically.

Bear in mind that the biggest negative events, and therefore the biggest energetic injuries, are causing the biggest problem, and that by repairing them we can create the biggest change in our energy system, and therefore the biggest change emotionally.

For each one relationship, you may be able to remember a few significant or stressful events. Probably the worst events are the ones you will recall the easiest. Take the memories one by one. Choose one. Tune back into that specific event, feel where the pain or pressure is, soften and flow in the usual way, testing and repeating until it's all released.

If there's so much and you don't know where to begin, a good question to start with might be: "If I had to live my life over and could skip one thing or one person, who/what would that be?" That's usually the biggest disturbance and a great place to start, but do get some help for this.

Another approach is to plot out a time-line of your life to include key ages, key relationships and key events, by headlines only. Give them an intensity score from 0 to 10. Start with the biggest, and then release the rest chronologically.

This may take a few sessions and some time, but it will get easier and faster to release as you go. Work with a partner for support if you wish and remember to seek the help of an EmoTrance Practitioner if you get overwhelmed and in too deep. EmoTrance works great by telephone, so you can always get the help you need wherever you are in the world.

Step by step you will start to feel lighter, brighter and freer. Your behaviour in your current relationships will start to change and you will feel more open and able to engage more deeply and freely with your partner.

Questions on Letting Go of the Painful Past

I have multiple pains when I recall the event. Which do I tackle first?

Choose the biggest one to release then go to the other one next.

When I focus on one energy, another one flares up somewhere else; then when I focus there, the first one flares up.

Try focusing on both simultaneously with the intention that both are softening and flowing.

It's releasing but taking ages to flow.

If the flow is slow, check the consistency of the energy, how viscous it is. Soften it some more, as it gets softer the speed will increase.

It's releasing but there's just so much of it. Can I speed it up?

Exercise continued on next page

Yes. Energy can release in an instant. The only thing that stops it is our limiting beliefs. Focus on the flow and releasing process and simply have the intention that it's flowing faster and faster. I like the 'sitting in a time machine' analogy; watching events go by in fast forward.

I've released it but feel exhausted.

So we are not done yet. Check out the location of this exhausted feeling. Soften and flow the energy here and see if that gets your energy flowing better.

I'm out of time, but know there's more to do. How do I close off?

You can set the process to run in the background. Let's say the current process is softening, or it might be flowing and releasing. Simply notice what's going on, have the intention that the process will continue as you take your attention away, and then let your unconscious mind get on with the rest.

Energy Masters Tip

Energy responds to thought immediately. The reason we can't let go is simply a psychological thing. "It's not possible," "I've had it so long." "What would life be like without this?" "I'm no good at this kind of thing." We can override all these limitations by simply having a stronger overriding desire to let it go.

Simply hold the intention and speak out loud that:

"Whatever this is about; however long I've had it; whatever purpose its been serving me and whatever the reason I can't seem to be able to release it yet; it is my sincere, heartfelt and overriding desire to let this go now."

Return to the energy and it will now soften and release.

principles themselves and you will create around you a network of mutual support to help yourselves to keep the flow going in your lives. I can't tell you how much it means to us to be able to pick up the phone to an ET Buddy when we are stuck and to not only have someone to listen, but someone to assist us to heal, release, transform and move on in minutes, so by the end of the call, we are free of that problem. To be able to be a real support to each other in life creates some very special friendships.

I Was Out of My Body With Fear

Sheila came to see me for help with her physical problems, but after she heard a talk I gave on the mind-body connection, she suspected that her emotional past might have something to do with her physical problems. She was in her 60s, had low energy, had a sadness about her, aches and pains in her limbs, poor circulation and throughout her life had suffered from lung infections and a prolapsed heart valve. Though the heart valve was apparently corrected now, she still continued to suffer circulation problems. She was worried about "digging up the past." When she had been to a counsellor, it was very painful and traumatic to revisit. Before getting into the details, I asked her, "When you discussed your childhood with your counsellor and visited the most painful part, what part of your body hurt most when you were talking about it?" She clutched her chest. "My heart," she said.

I reassured her that it would be possible to release her past without describing the intimate details to me unless she felt comfortable doing so. Before we started, I thought it would be a good idea to make chronological map of her past, with head-lines only, so we could see where to begin.

This was the map.

Age: 0 — 6 — 7 — 9 — 12 — — — — 16

Age 0: Born into family of domestic violence, her father had severe alcohol problems, her mother was manic–depressive. As an infant she was in and out of hospital with lung infections.

Age 5: Witnessed her mother plotting with a friend to beat up her father, felt powerless, yet guilty for doing nothing.

Age 6: Admitted to hospital with an unknown infection. Kept in isolation ward for 6 months. She had an "out of body experience" from fear of separation from her mother. Father started to visit her and she started to build relationship with him and learn the pattern that being sick gets you love.

Age 7: Father, having now built a relationship, "abandoned her" as he was taken away for rehabilitation for his problem.

Age 9: Witnesses brother taken away in a straight jacket.

Age 12: Father, who came back after rehab, had left again, leaving her abandoned and responsible for manic–depressive mother.

Age 16: Finally left home to live with Grandmother

We prioritised the events, scored them 0 through 10. There were several 10s. I asked, "If there was one event or person you could skip if you had your life to live over, what would that be?"

She replied, "When I was in the isolation ward and I had the out of body experience." So we started with that, the biggest energetic injury. This energy was in her heart, we softened and released it all until she could be completely peaceful about that memory. Step by step I asked her to focus on each of the other painful memories, by headline only, as opposed to going into details, then asked her where did she feel that in her body? The energy injuries were in the heart, the chest and in her arms and legs. It was easy to see how this chronically-held blocked energy all these years, in her heart, her lungs, her limbs, might have contributed to her physical problems in life. We had about six sessions together, setting her homework between each session to work on releasing aspects of the memories, and gradually her pains in the limbs disappeared, her energy grew stronger, her heart lighter, her depression and sadness lifted and she began to be happy and really start to enjoy her life. Sheila even started dancing.

CHAPTER 15

F orgiveness Made Easy

W hen healing the past, forgiveness is important for complete release. Not only forgiving those who did and said what they did, but forgiving yourself is the key to all forgiveness and the ability to love yourself fully. When healing the past, we often focus on healing what someone did to us and to forgiving them for what they did. But unless we also forgive ourselves for our part in the event, in the dynamic of what happened, then true healing may not completely take place. I am talking here of the:

- ✣ Why didn't I see it coming?

- ✣ I could have stopped it.

- ✣ Why did I get in that car?

- ✣ Why didn't I protect myself from this?

- ✣ I didn't do enough; its all my fault.

This unforgiveness, leads to self hatred and an apparent hatred of others—the others who trigger these old energetic injuries of self hate which clearly affect our future relationships.

When we can release the anger and guilt and self hate to ourselves for our part in the event, the anger and hate to the perpetrator often releases more easily.

Empty After Sex

When Jane was young she decided to "get rid" of her virginity. All her friends had lost their virginity and she didn't want to be the odd one out anymore. She decided to do this with an oily waiter she met in a Tapas bar. He took her to his flat. It was dirty and there was a filthy mattress. That unpleasant event left its injuries. She never enjoyed sex in later life. She felt empty and disconnected after sex. She loathed herself and believed that no good man would ever want her.

She had years of therapy, all directed at forgiving the oily waiter for what he had done and the squalid conditions in which it had taken place. But nothing changed her self loathing and her hatred of men until she forgave herself. Until she recognised that she had done that to herself, that she had chosen that. When she finally connected with the energy of her part in the event, it was in her throat, the "not telling him to stop" and a hard energy in her genital area. When she released this energy, she forgave herself and everything changed for her at last. No more did she accept boyfriends who treated her badly, (or she allowed to treat her badly). Out went the old boyfriend. Now she deserved better and could attract a different kind of partner as she could finally love herself more.

Gang Raped Beaten and Left for Dead

Susan had an invitation to get in a car with a group of drunken college boys, an event that led to her being gang raped, beaten and left for dead in a field. She was in therapy for years. Her symptoms were depression, self mutilation, inability to concentrate, psoriasis skin rash and she was registered disabled. Why did she get in the car? She didn't know what it would lead to but she knew she shouldn't have gotten in. In her energy system, she was responsible, she was guilty, she got in the car. We are not discussing who "is" responsible, only how it feels to the person involved. If in her energy system she feels guilty and responsible and unable to forgive herself, then this is the only reality that counts for her. Until she forgave herself for her decision, which led to the subsequent experience, she could not heal. But when she did, 35 years later, the forgiveness and the release of the rest of the trauma was easy and real change and transformation in her finally took place.

Once we can recognise the part we played and forgive ourselves for this, then releasing the rest of the trauma or painful memory is much easier. Actual forgiveness in the energy world view is easier than the complex psychological view. We simply ask them, "When you think of what you did or what you didn't do and you think of forgiving yourself for your part in this, where do you feel that in your body?" This connects us to the unforgiveness or guilt, which is an energy that we can then soften and release at last.

o More Tears!

*C*rying is a form of energy release. For many crying comes easily and is a great relief. For others crying was forbidden or understood to be a sign of weakness whilst growing up. The latter scenarios result in a more closed, contained and restrained energy system, and difficulties expressing or even connecting with emotions later in life—never mind releasing emotional energy.

In most cultures women are allowed to feel emotions while growing up and as an adult, which develops a more open energy system, functioning in a healthier way. Women know that they feel better after a good cry; however, we also know there are after effects: the puffy eyes, blotchy skin and exhaustion. Also, although we feel better, the problem is not always completely resolved, and can resurface again later.

So let's have a closer look at the energetics of this and explore how that emotional energy could be transformed and released more efficiently. I like this discovery a lot, because I'm one of those unfortunates who ends up with a face like a pomegranate and it takes three hours for my eyes to recover after a good cry!

When you've had an emotional release through crying, yes you have released some energy, but just like the flood gates opened and it all flowed out, there's a mess to clear up after the waters have subsided. The body has a half day clean up job to do to clear the debris!

Denser Energy Feels More Physical

If you have been doing the exercises along the way, you will have learned and experienced so far and that the denser the energy the stronger you feel it in your body as a physical sensation. Conversely, the lighter the energy, the less dense and the more easily and faster it flows and the lighter and more subtle the accompanying physical sensation.

So denser energy makes a stronger physical impact. It also moves more slowly. When the energy moves up the body into the head and we feel all that heavy pressure in the head and the tears are streaming, the energy is dense. It's moving, but it's dense; hence it's making a strong physical impact.

So whilst being able to cry is a great move forward for some who can't release emotional energy at all, I will now show you an even better and cleaner way to release that same energy. This might make those who don't cry easily more able to release that old energy now.

Transform Your Almost Tears into Light Mist

Next time you feel close to crying, as you feel that sensation of wanting to cry, pay attention. What's actually going on in the body? Where is the pressure? In the head? In the face? Behind the eyes? In the nose? How heavy or dense is it? Remind yourself what that is; it's all energy, only energy, and now we can soften that. Have the intention for the energy to soften and flow; hold your attention there and watch and feel that energy become softer and lighter. The lighter it becomes the easier it flows. It can even vaporise off you—that's how I experience it.

You release the same emotional energy, but now you are light, fresh and clear. No aftermath of the flood to clear up. It's like the flood water got vaporised on its way out so everything in its path is left intact and clean. No puffy eyelids, no blotchy skin, no exhaustion—just lightness, freshness, clarity, peace and joy. Now that is cool!

Whilst you are working on the painful past, remember that the energy behind crying is still only energy releasing in a denser way. Just do an experiment the next time the energy moves up into your head and eyes that way, and see how that works for you. We are, in fact, our own research lab. That's how I discovered this for myself, a kind of experiment at first, with a great result, which is now a common practice that works for others as well as me.

Also, when working with a partner or a client and they burst into tears, realise what's happening. They are tuned in to the emotion of what's going on; e.g. the sadness and loss, and the energy is dense. To get your partner to focus back onto what's actually going on in their body and to engage them in softening that energy is not only a faster way to work with them, but it's also a kinder way. Wouldn't you rather be experiencing a physical sensation moving through and releasing out of your body than the emotion of deep sadness?

Just an after note: crying is ok. It works and does the job, though not 100 percent and it can be a bit messy and take longer. We now have another way to release that same energy, faster, more cleanly AND more completely.

Once you have experienced this and know that you can do it, you may congratulate yourself indeed for your developing mastery over your energy system.

CHAPTER 17

I Love Him, But...

I could also call this ... 'I love him/her BUT.....' and that BUT can be:

- ✎ 'When he leaves his stuff everywhere it drives me crazy'
- ✎ 'When he goes humph in that judging and knowing way, I can't stand it'
- ✎ 'When she gets all emotional I can't take it, I have to remove myself from her presence'
- ✎ 'When he's angry I shake and tremble and can't respond'
- ✎ 'When someone gets confrontational with me, it really makes me angry'
- ✎ 'I can't stand her negative moaning'
- ✎ 'The way she never stops talking just drains me; five minutes is my max and I've gotta go'
- ✎ 'When she won't do as I say and I can't get through, I get so angry'
- ✎ 'I cannot abide bad language or insolent remarks'

I am sure you get the picture and I am also sure there are many more behaviours that cause you to lose your connection with you partner or loved one and so disrupt the flow of energy and of love.

So far you may be blaming *Them* for *Their* behaviour that's causing *You* a problem. Now you are this far into the book, you have passed the point of no return. There is no more blame. There is only *Your* responsibility for *Your* emotions, recognising Your discomfort is about *Your* ability right now to handle that kind of energy. This kind of energy coming along is the perfect opportunity for you to develop yourself, to develop the capacity and strength, and the ability to handle it and therefore to grow as a person.

Let me share with you a couple of examples of the benefits of making the effort to do this or getting some help to do this. There are more in Section 3: Inspiring Stores of Healing and Love starting on page 163. The resolution of the original problems and difficulties all demonstrate the principle of 'energy needs to flow' and 'everyone needs energy nutrition.'

Someone Who Drains You

My Grandmother was a character, but she could talk for England. She was Irish and yes she had kissed the Blarney stone! Though I'm not sure that's what was behind it! Anyway, she was intense and with time, because of this intense demanding of people's attention, as most couldn't handle it, they only visited her for a short time and would leave exasperated and then stay away. You can imagine that for her, not receiving what she needed only intensified the problem. I was no different from anyone else until I understood about transforming emotional energy with EmoTrance. The next time I was sitting chatting with her, and came to the point of "Right that's it I've got to go" which was only after about 10 minutes, I asked myself "Why? Why am I feeling so uncomfortable that I have to leave? Where is this discomfort in my body?" Interesting, I found a pressure building in my stomach. So I allowed it to soften, for the energy to release, for me to be comfortable once again. The process was totally invisible to my Grandmother of course and I became quite happy once again and able to sit longer listening to her and giving her the attention and acceptance that she needed from another human being. The dynamic also changed for her. Instead of craving my attention as she was so lacking, having now been able to satisfy that craving she became a normal reasonable entertaining wonderful woman to chat with. I learned a lot through that experiment about why people crave that attention by really allowing that person in, to understand what that was about, to transform my impatience, frustration and exasperation into the joy and love in the relationship with my dear Grandmother.

This is an important point about how we respond to attention-seeking behaviour. "Don't pander to it," is our normal response, but this only perpetuates and makes the energetic problem more severe. Silvia Hartmann observed this energetic dynamic when working with animals with attention-seeking behaviour in her years as a dog trainer. She found that giving them what they needed at the time they needed it, was actually the way to resolve the problem. Attention-seeking behaviour arose from an energetic deficiency in social animals who don't receive enough social interaction. The Harmony Programme (www.a1harmony.com) that she developed in 1993 for animal behaviour problems was actually the precursor to EmoTrance.

Anger and Confrontation

This was something I used to struggle with a lot so I'd like to share an experience of how things used to be and then how things became after I learned how to transform emotional energy.

I was working hard and was away from the office a lot, seeing private clients, working away over long weekend training courses, and catching up best I could in the office with the marketing team. One day my Admin Officer came into my office, slammed her folder down on my desk and out came an angry complaint about how I'd been taking her for granted, how hard she works, how little she was paid, and that if I didn't do something about it she was leaving. She knew what a mess that would leave us in. She stood there angrily waiting for my response. I was in shock. I was so taken by surprise and totally lost for words. I muttered something like "Leave it with me" so she would leave my office. And I sat shaking, my stomach churning and my face hot and flushed. No-one had ever spoken to me like that before, except maybe an angry parent when I was a child.

I took a few deep breaths and managed to pick up the phone to my consultant friend who was helping me in the business. I told him what happened. I felt weak and pathetic, couldn't even think clearly and didn't know what to do. I certainly couldn't meet her salary demands. He offered to handle it for me, but tempting though it was I thought, "Get a grip girl, you need to be able to handle this stuff better than that. Walk the talk." So that evening I spent some time recalling what happened, releasing all that energy in my body. That was an improvement. I continued practising handling even stronger anger, stronger confrontation, breathing all that energy in through and out till I felt so much stronger. I called her back in my office the next day for a chat. It was a completely difference interaction. She was still angry and defiant. I asked her to tell me again what's going on for her, what she wants and how she's feeling.

I listened, I absorbed it all. I let her finish before I spoke. I was completely relaxed and was able to 'see' totally where she was coming from, 'understand completely' her situation and point of view. "You're right of course; I have been taking you for granted. You do work hard, you are extremely loyal and talented, and I have depended on that while I've been away so much. Yes, you deserve to be paid more than you are. I'm sure I would be feeling exactly the same way if I were in your shoes." I felt her energy totally release and diffuse. Myself, I was relaxed, clear, compassionate, confident and strong. I was able to respond much more resourcefully as I had the clarity I needed. Her defences came down; her anger diffused we were now able to have a reasonable discussion about what I and the business could do to meet her needs given the limitations of the business. We reached a mutually acceptable compromise. We were both happy again; the crisis had been resolved.

This is 'energy needs to flow' and 'everyone needs energy nutrition' in action.

Once I was able to accept her energy, I could genuinely understand what it was all about and see her point of view. Through me being able to accept her energy and give her some recognition and appreciation in return (that little soothing balm of energy nutrition always helps) we were able to create an outcome and resolve the problem, which could not have been reached before and strengthen our own relationship by having been able to be so open and honest with each other.

What did I get? A lot more than a happy team member. I got real changes within. I got new strength and development of my personal capacity to handle this kind of energy in a relaxed, comfortable, resourceful and compassionate way. That has stayed with me ever since, and that has given me the power and resources to diffuse other situations in a similar way and teach others how to do the same.

So now it's your turn. Work through Exercise 7: Handling Difficult Behaviours, and you will discover the simple principles are always at work in the solution: Energy Needs to Flow and Everyone Needs Energy Nutrition.

Handling Difficult Behaviours

You can do this with a partner or on your own.

Look at your relationships, your partner, your family, your work colleagues.

Note what behaviours you find difficult to handle right now.

Write them down so you can work through them.

Contemplate for a moment the impact in your life of this dynamic that's going on, how it's affecting your relationship right now.

For each behaviour:

- Think of that behaviour from that person, then notice what you feel in your body.

- Soften flow and release the energy.

- Test: Again, think of that behaviour, find the energy disturbances, soften, flow and release.

- A partner may help by role playing the behaviour for you and reminding you to locate and soften the energy.

- Test and repeat until you are clear.

Energy Mastery Tips:

- Remember there are ways of speeding the energy release process up, simply by having the intention that it's flowing faster, then just watch it all rush out.

- Another way to speed up the softening process is to introduce another energy into the area you want to soften. In EmoTrance we use the energy of water for its dissolving flowing and cleansing properties. Simply imagine that water is flowing into the energy and watch what happens. In other words, we invoke the energy of water. This usually helps to soften resistant energy and to help flush it away. Personally I find the energy of 'magic water' works every time! We are using the principle that 'intention influences energy immediately.'

Resistance is only a human psychological limitation. There are various ways of overcoming these limitations—and this is one. We just have to think what we want and it happens immediately in the energy realms.

I strongly recommend you do this next step:

Exercise continued on next page

Getting energised

- For whatever behaviour you were working with, imagine you have double that to handle.

- Get your partner to do or say the behaviour if it makes it more real for you.

- Or imagine that you have so much more of it to handle.

- Breathe it all in, soften and let it flow through you and out.

- Think of it flowing really fast.

- Take it in again, even more if you can until you feel energised.

- You may find you are laughing about it now.

- Ask yourself, or get your partner to ask you:

- How do you feel in the face of that behaviour now?

- How do you respond to that behaviour now?

- Will the person in question be able to handle your new responses better than your old response?

- Can you see how you can change the dynamic and outcome now for yourself, at the same time, developing and growing in strength and capacity yourself?

- Can you see that life has brought you exactly what you needed to learn, and grow from, once you could accept it?

- Observe your new behaviour in those relationship situations from now on.

If there is anything else that comes up when you're in the real situation, as opposed to the simulated situation, then try softening and flowing in the moment. If you can't do that, then make a note to do repair your energy system later.

CHAPTER 18

Shields and Barriers to Love and Life

*M*any of us have strong defences and are not open and trusting enough to receive when another pays us a compliment or offers us love. We are suspicious; it's too risky, we were hurt before, and we just won't let someone in again until we are absolutely sure it's safe. This stems from injuries to our energy system sustained in a past experience. Something happened and is still stored in our energy system. We know it. We can feel it. It hurts when we let life in to touch it. Yet despite being closed and guarded we are still looking for, and even craving the joy of love in our life.

While we are closed, injured and afraid, protecting ourselves from yet more injury we cannot experience the real highs and the deep nourishment that is available to us when we let the energy of people in. When we 'feel' love for something or a person, what we are feeling is a flow of energy through us that makes us feel so good. It's a real physical sensation in the body. We have to be open in some way to let that person or experience in. When that energy of life and love streams through us we feel it both physically and emotionally. Every cell tingles; warm and alive with joy and delight. But often those shields and barriers leave us numb. Life is ok, but its far from amazing.

Shields and barriers are real energetic devices that we use, consciously or unconsciously, to hold back certain energies that we cannot handle at the moment. The energy of the shield and the energies beyond the shield are outside of the body and in our wider energy field and beyond. Not allowing those energies in means we feel nothing. We can think of the person or the subject and we feel numb. It's not real for us. We may even feel empty. We may feel that nothing affects us, 'we have no issues or problems to solve' because in fact nothing touches us. It's true: literally, nothing gets in through those barriers!

The problem with these shields is that although they are serving a purpose, holding back energies that we fear will hurt us, they also result in us holding back a lot of other positive energies of life. This means we are malnourished energetically; lacking in energy vitamins, so to speak. This often results in behaviours that seek out nourishment from other sources. This may be in our need for love and recognition in relationships, or in our work. It may even mean we seek that nourishment in addictive

behaviours, addictive because we are never satisfied truly, due to our energy barriers and injuries, which stop that steady flow of nourishing life energies.

We may be shielded to certain people. It may be certain behaviours in people. Beliefs can also be shields. The 'I cannot accept such a thing to be true' is an energy shield. Strong avoidance behaviours also indicate shields.

The following true story illustrates how we approach shields and the great benefits of us dismantling them, albeit in a safe controlled way.

Christine Was Numb

Christine came to see me because for some time she was numb to life. She couldn't feel anything in her life. She had no emotions. Her sister had cancer, and even for this she felt nothing. She wanted to be able to feel her emotions again; to feel alive again.

"How long has this been going on," I asked her.

"About four years."

"What was going on four years ago?

"I went through a messy and painful divorce. I got to my limit of what I could take and shut down, closed off and retreated to my ivory tower. It helped me cope, but I've been like this since then."

So Christine was handling a lot of stressful events back then. Being unable to handle so much energy building up inside and getting stuck—it was just too painful. Shutting down was a way to consciously or unconsciously create an energy shield to hold back the energies of her husband, which were triggering much pain in her. So now we knew what her shield was holding back originally, but she was numb to everything, so it was also holding back a lot of other life energies. Before we could think about taking down the shield we had to do some repairs in her energy system, the energetic injuries sustained by events that happened four years earlier.

This is how our session went.

Sandra: Imagine your husband was way over there somewhere (pointing out into the distance) and was approaching. How close could he come before you started to get uncomfortable?

Christine: Stop there, outside the room.

She clutched at her throat and leaned backwards. Christine was feeling tight in the throat.

Sandra: Ok, push him away a bit so you're comfortable.

Now we had located where the energy shield was, outside her body, at a distance just outside the room, holding her husband's energy away from her.

Sandra: What we will do in a moment is make tiny hole in that shield that is holding all his energy back, and allow the tiniest thread of his energy to flow towards you. You will allow it in, let it flow through you and out and just see what that feels like; a taste, if you like, of that energy. How do you feel about that?

Christine was clutching her throat and I could see that her skin was flushed there. We had to release this resistance first.

Sandra: Ok so focus on this feeling in your throat, allow it to soften and flow, and tell me where it wants to go.

It released down through her chest, right arm, and out of her hand. Christine's resistance was now gone and she was ready to have a taste of his energy. So we

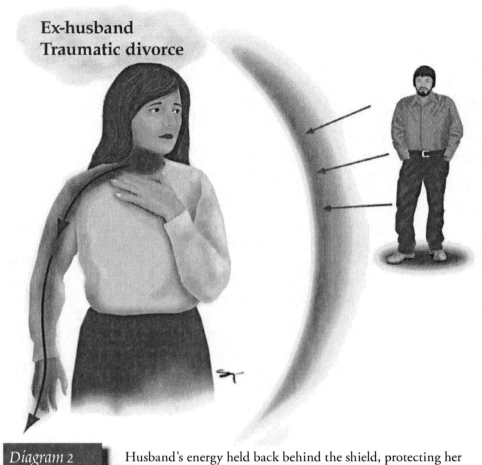

**Ex-husband
Traumatic divorce**

Diagram 2

Husband's energy held back behind the shield, protecting her from energetic injuries in the throat. Inner injuries are healed and energy releases through chest and out via right arm.

made the tiny hole and allowed a thin thread of his energy through. It arrived at her throat, as she felt it tighten again. So again we soften and released it. Then we increasingly took more and more of her husband's energy, increasing the hole size in comfortable increments, and the energy flowed in new paths in her body, getting stuck in her chest and stomach, causing discomfort. We softened and released all the areas that felt uncomfortable till all was flowing. Eventually, she was able to handle all of her husband's energy and the whole atmosphere in the room had changed. The energy was so soft and light. Love filled the room.

Sandra: How do you feel now?

Christine: I just feel love. I feel love for him again.

Sandra: And how do you feel now when you think of your sister and her cancer?

Christine: I just feel love for her.

This transformation lasted. A few weeks later I had cause to speak to Christine on the phone and she said she felt open, reconnected, felt her emotions again and was happy they had come back.

This session illustrates a number of important learning points.

- ↝ We used a little of her husband's energy to find and trigger the old injuries in the body so we could heal them and restore energy flow, allowing her to progressively be able to handle more and more of his energy.

- ↝ We didn't have to know what actually happened four years earlier, who said what, who did what. This speeds the whole process up and is comfortable way to work for that person.

- ↝ The disconnection she had made with her husband had disconnected her from other life experiences and made her numb.

- ↝ Releasing this shield reconnected her with life again.

- ↝ What she was holding back so strongly, actually brought her maximum benefit, namely Love, when she was able to handle it.

- ↝ The greater the flow in her energy system the stronger the feeling of Love.

- ↝ Note also that when thinking of her sister she didn't feel pain, she felt Love; i.e. she had the capacity to handle her sister's situation.

- ↝ There is great value, energy nourishment and benefit to be had from what is behind our shields, great learning, which we cannot access while those shields are there.

There are more stories of reconnection and healing from the release of shields elsewhere in the book showing the changes in our behaviours, our perspective and our life when we now start to receive that nourishment, which we held back from us. Releasing our shields is one of the best things we can do for ourselves. See the following stories in Section 3 for deeper understanding and inspiration.

- ↝ The Stalker Brought Me Strength and Backbone (page 167)

- ↝ I Couldn't Say "I Love You" To My Dad (page 168)

- ↝ From Fear and Resistance to Excitement About a New Job (page 171)

- ↝ Ecstasy and Oneness on the Subway (page 175)

Releasing Your Own Shields

The energetic injuries and hurts that are behind our shields are often quite severe, and you will benefit from having some help so that you can repair those injuries and take down the shields gently and comfortably. This is something I would recommend doing with an EmoTrance Practitioner or with a partner, once they have had plenty of practice of working with transforming emotional energy in the earlier exercises. If you decide to attempt this yourself, and get into deep waters, then close up any hole in the shield, soften, flow and release any energy you took in, and seek the help of a practitioner in order to complete the work (Exercise 8: Releasing Shields).

Alternatively, you may wish to attend the EmoTrance Practitioner Training yourself and learn in a safe environment.

To find an EmoTrance Practitioner, *see* Additional Resources on page 191.

I Couldn't Love My Baby

Last night I watched an excellent documentary on TV's Channel 4 about a woman who couldn't love her new baby. The birth was premature and traumatic, and the mother had no connection with the new born. She went into a postnatal depression, feeling numb. The disconnection from her baby had an effect on the baby too. The baby couldn't look her mother in the eye, and always looked away—the disconnected blankness of its mother obviously triggering pain for the baby she couldn't handle. The mother and child received therapy and help. It took 12 months of conventional therapy to restore the connection, and still there were a few unresolved issues. Birthdays, instead of being a happy occasions, brought conflicting emotions because they were also an anniversary of an unresolved birth trauma. The baby was still insecure if left for any length of time, invoking for the baby the early traumas of being left unattended without her mother's touch.

I watched the film observing the energy dynamics. The initial trauma of the birth could have been released as a painful memory. The disconnection with the baby could have been released by finding and releasing the mother's shield to her baby. Also, as we will see later in Exercise 24: Assisting Another (page 151), understanding how the baby's early traumas could also have been released energetically by proxy, would allow the baby to grow up with a stronger sense of security, without that energetic memory of abandonment.

All of this is so easy with EmoTrance. Although conventional therapy obviously helps, we now have knowledge and tools that can accelerate the therapeutic process and alleviate people's suffering so much faster.

EmoTrance gives us a beautiful simple natural way to repair our energy system of these old injuries, to safely release our shields and barriers so that we can be more

Releasing Shields

This is an exercise to do with a partner, preferably experienced in transforming energy, ideally an EmoTrance Practitioner. Should you wish to try this with a partner at home, these are the steps for the facilitator.

Identify the shield

Is it a person, a concept, a situation, or a behaviour partner avoids. Have the partner check out the relationships around them by thinking of an open loving connection and note the immediate response. The strong "no way" reaction accompanied by defensive body language indicates a possible shield.

Locate the shield

Get your partner to imagine the person, behaviour or concept far away. Then let it approach. Ask how close it can come before your partner feels uncomfortable? Now you've located the shield.

Clear any resistance to tackling this

Tell your partner what you are going to do before you do it, and ask what they feel in their body; i.e. "We are going to allow a tiny bit of that energy in to see what it feels like and to let it go. What do you feel in your body about that?" There is often resistance to clear before commencing. Soften and release until the partner is ready.

Use a tiny thread of energy to trigger energy injuries in your partner's body so that they can repair them by softening and flowing. Open a pin prick hole in the shield and invite that energy in. Where does it enter? How does that feel? Do they need to soften and flow? Where else does it want to go? Have your partner describe the path through and out of the body. Soften and flow any areas of discomfort on the way. Check if that feels comfortable before increasing the 'in' flow.

Energy Mastery Tip

If the flow slows down, the energy has become heavier and more viscous. If you don't want to be there all afternoon, pay attention to the consistency of the flow with the intention that it softens some more so the flow will accelerate. Only when each amount of energy can be handled with ease, in, through and out, should you attempt to increase the amount of incoming energy.

At the level of comfort of your partner, slowly increase the energy flow into the body. This could be by metaphorically taking out bricks one by one, making more holes, or making the hole bigger. If the flow becomes too much to handle, you can reduce the hole size, or slow down or close the energy flow, giving you a chance to clear what your partner has to deal with.

Once the shield is down and your partner can handle that energy, discuss what that means to them, and discuss how they might test their new behaviour now.

Always remember, the shield belongs to the person, and they control the pace at which you progress.

open, more courageous, more trusting and reconnect with the world and start to receive the nourishment that we crave.

Because there are good reasons for these barriers, we approach releasing shields in a very gentle, respectful and comfortable pace. I recommend that you do this with a qualified practitioner, but feel free to explore approaching this yourself.

Why Do I Always Fall for the Wrong Guy?

Helen was a telephone client I had today. She said, "I always end up loving someone who doesn't love me back," and was starting to feel emotional as she spoke; the energy welling up in her chest. This was a person who was an excellent judge of character in general, had very good open trusting relationships with women, animals and gay men, but when it came to heterosexual men, she was disconnected, made bad judgements, wrong interpretations of events and generally didn't have much success.

We softened and flowed and managed to get this energy flowing down through her stomach and a thin flow down the legs and out. She went on to say that the idea of looking at someone you love and knowing that they don't love you, produced a weird feeling in the heart and a sense of a barrier outside holding that energy of someone looking at her, as it was too painful to accept.

We released the energy in the heart area then started to introduce a little of that male energy bit by bit through the shield. As it came in, there was another shield inside her body, spinning and diffusing the incoming energy so it didn't get further down to the injured areas below. We softened all the obstacles along the way. Some of the resistances were fears; such as "If I let him in, somehow I'll end up pregnant" or "I'll be taken advantage of." Gradually Helen was able to stand in front of a guy and take that energy in completely: into her heart, through her body and out. It felt warm and nice. It had nothing to do with sex and was completely non-threatening. She realised that she could let a man's energy in and actually read that energy and all the information it contained, and enjoy the experience of it.

It dawned on her actually how much safer it was to be more open energetically. This way she could now truly read a person and their intentions, as opposed to just listening to their words. By being open she had now repaired those old injuries, so far from making foolish judgements and assessments, they were more likely to be accurate. She had the realisation that even if a guy had liked her before, her own defences had disconnected her from him and from any possible deeper heart enriching experience ever happening in the relationship. Even if they had sex it was in a disconnected way. And if a guy did actually like her, she couldn't actually feel it because she didn't let that energy in, which gave her the experience and pain that they didn't love her in return.

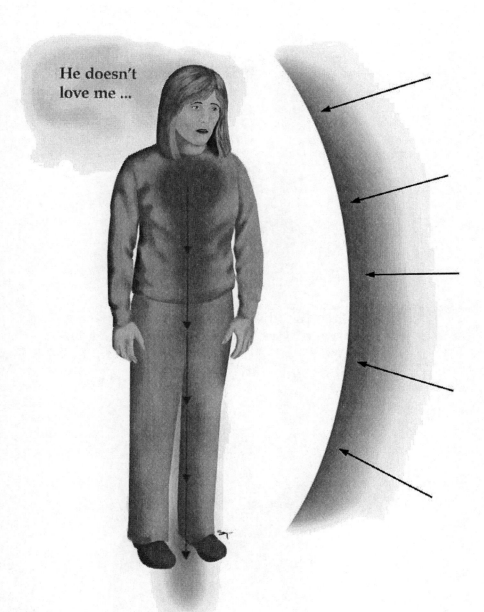

Diagram 4 Some energy allowed through outer shield, hits inner shield, deflecting energy again from deeper Energetic injuries.

Diagram 5 Eventually all inner injuries healed, shield broken down and all energy allowed to flow in through and out.

This was a complete revelation for Helen. So, with the old injuries now repaired, her barriers down, her heart energy channel now open and flowing, she is ready to explore her male relationships in a whole new way.

We set some homework to practice connecting with men, allowing their energy in fully through the open heart channel, reading it in her whole energy matrix, and letting it go and to enjoy and learn from that experience. This was important for Helen, as we had just done an exercise in a therapeutic context, but the real test would be in real life. If any old barriers were triggered with men, especially if she found them attractive, she could now be aware of that and would soften and flow, and keep her heart open. Living like this, with that heart channel open in itself would lead to very different opportunities for relationships and their development, making her life quite different now, with enjoyable heart-warming experiences with men replacing the previous nervous experiences. Helen's first feedback to me was great and she is delighted with the new world of possibilities that has opened up for her. The homework is detailed in Exercise 9: Guaranteed Energy High Night Out (page 62).

Guaranteed Energy-High Night Out

Plan a night out with a friend who has read this book and who, like you, knows how to transform energy. Wherever you decide to go, a club, bar or restaurant, experiment with opening your heart channel and inviting in people's energy and really feeling it then letting it go.

Notice different qualities about different people's energy. Notice how it makes you feel when you really let that flow though you. If you can't do this easily, practice with a friend until you can accept their energy easily and fully, and let it go. It should feel good. If it doesn't yet, or the flow's not strong enough, soften and flow the blocked areas to increase the flow.

If you are still shielded and feeling unsafe to do this exercise, then do some preparatory shield release work beforehand.

You will find some people's energy makes you warm and fuzzy, some make you feel sparkly, some are really energizing. Do it with a few people and your own energy state will build and build until you feel really amazing. Then you can shine all that energy right back!

If appropriate, share with someone what you got from their energy once you've really felt it. Anyone would be happy to learn how great their energy feels. Say it like it is, from the heart:

"I hope you don't mind me saying, but you have a really sparkling energy and it makes me feel really great—thank you!" It will absolutely make someone's day!

Enjoy, and let us know, through our website, how you got on!

"What comes from the heart goes directly
and easily to the heart of the other."

Old Egyptian Saying

CHAPTER 19

Change Your Beliefs, Change Your World

*Y*ou often hear people say, "I cannot accept that" or "I have to see it to can believe it." We need the evidence before we can trust. People searching for religious or spiritual experience are looking for evidence before they can believe, and we have the concept of 'leap of faith;' i.e. we have to believe and then we can have the experience! i.e. we have to trust. What is going on energetically here?

Barriers to Belief

Trust is openness and acceptance. This allows certain energies to flow in, which couldn't before. When the energy can flow in, our spirit person can 'experience it' in the real. We feel it; something happens.

You might also then explore applying this approach to something that you are resisting as truth, for whatever reason, or refusing to accept. Do it as an exploration exercise, following the approach set out in Exercise 8: Releasing Shields (page 57).

Beliefs are Energetic

Notice that beliefs themselves are energetic in nature. They are formed through learning; i.e. we take this information or energy that someone tells us to be true inside and we hold onto that. For example, "The doctor said I will have to live with this," "Children should be seen and not heard." It's an energy state. They are formed also through experience. We have an experience—that's an energetic event. Life happens, we experience it in a certain way; i.e. the energy flows in and we handle it within our energy system in a certain way. If we didn't release that experience fully, to get the full transformation of that experience; e.g. the energy got stuck and it was challenging in some way. This may attract a similar handling of the next experience. The energy disturbance within becomes more dense and forming a belief.

Here's a personal example. I recall doing some calculations one time and discovered later that I had made some mistakes. On another occasion I was doing something else similar and it turned out I had made another mistake. Now I'm starting to form the belief that I'm no good at calculations, which is really crazy, since I recall my A Level Applied Maths exam (when I was 18) being the best exam I ever did and when I was 15 and had a Saturday job on the market I could hold and add a long string of numbers together in my head so easily! But this new reality was starting to persist.

Now, if I was in flow at the time in the first event, I would have had the clarity to not have had the mistake experience, which I held onto and which grew into a belief. So the reality that I continued to live out and manifest in my life as that belief continued to limit my accuracy in that kind of task. We manifest what we believe because we don't fully process and release our experience. So the energy of future life events get filtered through our complex energetic patterning to manifest the same reality.

But it's all energy, only energy. So now when we discover our limiting beliefs such as "It's hard," "It's not possible," "I can't do that," "It's incurable," "People like me don't have such experiences in life," "I'm not good enough," we can simply ask: "Where do I feel that?" Check inside and outside your body. Energy needs to flow in, through and out. So breathe, soften and flow, and release those limitations. Open yourself and your life up to new possibilities and different experiences: a life without those limits.

Releasing a Belief to Enhance Performance

Beliefs are not always shields outside the body. I now find the reason I have not released my limiting belief about maths in all this time is so that I can do it now to show you the steps as an illustration!

When I say "I'm no good at math" I feel a sensation in my stomach. The level of how true that statement is, is 7/10 right now. So, I soften and flow. The energy flows downwards into the legs, seems to slow down in the thighs, need to soften a bit more for it to flow there, and now it's released. So now I say "I'm good at maths" and I believe that to be true 8/10. So there's still a little remaining lack of belief. Where do I feel that? That's at the top of my head. So I soften and the energy releases outwards from my head. Now I am good at maths and it's a 9/10. I do a test writing down a list of three- and four-digit numbers that normally I would use a calculator for. I can do that, and as I do, I feel a slight sensation again in my head, subtle, but allowing slight loss of clarity. Again, soften and flow. Now I test once more with all kinds of strings of numbers and I can add them up correctly in my head without a calculator. So now I ask, how much do I still need to rely on my calculator; i.e. how much do I trust my accuracy? There's still a slight sensation in my stomach. Soften and flow and release. Ok, "I am good at calculations" that's a 10/10. Let's try: "I am great at calculations." There is some resistance in my chest. Soften and flow. "I am brilliant at calculations;" something in my shoulders, soften and flow. Now I feel very confident and happy and energised about calculations. I have created greater flow for this task. My definition of brilliant may be very different from someone else's. But I think you get the idea of how the principle applies and how you can release the energy disturbances to create flow; i.e. release the resistances which is releasing our limitations.

This approach can be applied to any belief and any task you wish to perform or any area of your life. The limitations you have are only those energy patterns and disturbances that you now choose to hold onto.

CHAPTER 20

*F*ear Of Commitment

*D*on was a "ladies man." When a woman wanted to take their relationship to the next level, they would never hear from him again. He was 36 and was beginning to be tired of not having a home and his own family, but as soon as a woman would get that look in her eye, or start gazing at the jewellery stores, he was out of there faster than a speeding bullet.

His reputation with his past women was bad. He was a bit of a "love rat." He tried to justify this to himself by considering himself a fun-loving guy, but he had come to the conclusion that there was more to it and came to seek some help from an EmoTrance practitioner about his huge fear of commitment.

The practitioner asked him to remember the last time he saw that look in a woman's eye and to tell her exactly what he was feeling in his body and where it was. Don said he got a clenching pain in his lower abdomen, a tightness in his stomach and a sense of not being able to breathe easily or being unable to find his words. It was so uncomfortable that he really had to get away and not meet her again. Sometimes it happened after making love and at that point he would leave and not come back. He had never told anyone about this physical sensations he had before.

The practitioner explained it him that it was only energy; that it wasn't his fault, he wasn't a bad person. This energy was actually causing him to exhibit this behaviour towards women. They thought he was a bad guy. He felt guilty about that. But something in his energy system was causing this behaviour.

So the practitioner guided Don to focus on the energy and think of it softening. Where did it want to go? Upwards. As it flowed up, he felt a tight band across his stomach. The energy needed a lot of softening before it could flow further upward. Then it stuck in his throat. They softened the energy some more until finally he felt that it flowed up and out through his mouth.

They tested. Now remembering that look in her eyes, how did it feel? This time it was different, but he had a kind of nervous energy through his body. He got up walked about shaking his arms and shoulders and as directed, continued to soften and flow the energy which was now flowing better through his body, though it was still a bit stuck in the shoulders.

Testing again: there was still a tiny twinge in the lower abdomen, so more softening was required. Then an insight. He said, "This is to do with my father. He left when he found out Mum was pregnant, she has never heard from him since." There was some energy now blocked in the heart, which they softened and it released. Don now felt much better now and finally understood why he was the way he was.

So they were half way there. Don had been thinking of a particular woman who he had liked during this session. Now when he saw that look in her eye, the energy came in higher up, into his heart and flowed then up into his head. What he got now was an actual recognition of admiration and love from another person. Now it was feeling warmer and nice, though there was still a sense of, "Am I worthy? After all I've done, who I am? My Father didn't even want to know me." This energy was sticking at the back of his neck causing heaviness in his shoulders. They softened the energy and it slid away. He had never wanted to bear that heavy burden of being the man of the house in the absence of his father.

Now, back to the girl and the idea of actually being able to have love, a wife, a home and his own family. At this idea, the energy was now stronger, warmer and more energising. He felt immensely pleased. Don said he thought he might call her and apologise to her if that was OK. The practitioner said yes, that might be a good idea.

She also told Don to observe his reactions over the next week or so and notice if there was any remaining energy that needed to clear. They had released and opened new pathways and it would be good to keep the heart open now and consciously allow himself to feel those energies and keep them flowing.

Don was extremely grateful. Now it was actually possible for him to have love, a home and a family that he wouldn't leave.

This is an interesting case from a number of perspectives. From the woman's perspective, men who behave this way are "heartless bastards" and have caused a lot of hurt and anger in others by this behaviour. But there is always a reason for everything. If instead of reacting from anger, we are able to handle that energy, to accept absorb, digest and release the energy, to transform the hurt and pain, we might gain some understanding about what that behaviour or energy is about. There is a reason that a person cannot commit. That reason is an injury in their energy circuitry that makes it either painful or unacceptable for them to enter further along this path to deeper love and connection. From the male perspective, remember, our behaviour follows our energy state and the way our energy system is functioning in response to life. This is an opportunity to explore why it is we cannot or will not make a commitment towards a deeper connection in our relationship. What's going on in our energy body to create this behaviour? We can change this if we choose.

CHAPTER 21

Reconciliation or Divorce

elationships start out well, but things can go wrong. Even the smallest things can build up: lack of consideration, not paying enough attention when it's needed, words said in anger or stress, inability to handle certain behaviours, and even life events outside the relationship which take their toll on one partner can affect the energy dynamics of the relationship. Flow stops, one disconnects and the other can't get through anymore and is no longer heard. This can cause escalation in behaviours to try to get through and to be heard, like anger, raised voices or even aggression. If that gets through it often causes more injuries in the receiver so often the consequences are even stronger defences or a counter attack as a defence.

We continue to live out the menial practical level of life and avoid the 'issues,' avoid actually engaging with each other as it's too uncomfortable. We lose that heart connection, that openness and loving feeling with each other.

We can arrive at a point where we feel there's nothing left for us in a relationship. We can't get through anymore, or we just handle all the stress. We're not getting anything in return so we decide to separate for survival or to find what we need elsewhere.

Relationships fail because

ॐ energy stops flowing and we start hurting; and

ॐ energy nutrition is not happening anymore; we aren't getting what we need.

For those who are looking for a relationship, you will have the wonderful opportunity exploring how that relationship can develop, grow and deepen by applying the principles of energy flow and energy nutrition in this book. Other parts of this book, such as Chapter 24: Allowing Yourself to Fall in Love (page 80) and Chapter 26: Feeding Your Love (page 92) and the stories in Section 3: Inspiring Stories of Healing and Love (page 163) relate just how wonderful and rewarding that can be.

But if you are your hurting or uncomfortable or stressed in your relationship, or its gone stale and you're not being nourished and feeling loved, there is hope here. If you have already separated there is still hope of reconciliation.

All it takes for the energy dynamic of a relationship to change is for one person's energy system to change and work differently—then the relationship starts to work differently.

What we have control of is how our own energy system works. So what we need to do for ourselves is to restore the flow in our own energy system. Then we get some clarity, we get our resourcefulness back, we feel better, and we can start to change our own behaviour.

Do the following exercises to create the changes you want:

ᔌ Exercise 6: Letting Go of the Painful Past (page 37)

ᔌ Exercise 7: Handling Difficult Behaviours (page 49)

ᔌ Exercise 15: Heart Healing and Nutrition (page 116)

You can try these exercises alone or with a friend to guide you, or with an EmoTrance Practitioner.

With flow restored within ourselves, and remembering the principles that are also true for our partner, that Energy Needs to Flow and Everyone Needs Energy Nutrition, reconciliation is very possible and in itself is transforming and enriching for our relationships. Remember our partner needs to be accepted and they need attention, recognition and appreciation just like you do.

Separation to Reconciliation

Sue and John had separated already when Sue came to see me for a health overhaul. The relationship had grown stale over a two-year period and though John still wanted to be with Sue, she was unsure about what she wanted and had a total block when it came to physical intimacy. After the session, the couple got back together and happily restored their physical relationship. Here's the gist of the session with Sue which took us about 40 minutes.

Sandra: What do you want in relation to your husband?

Sue: I don't know.

Sandra: And where do you feel that in your body when you think 'I don't know'?

Sue: In my stomach.

Sandra guides Sue to use her intention to soften the energy in her stomach. The energy spreads and starts to flow downwards to her legs and out her feet.

Sandra: Ok. Now, what do you want?

Sue: I want to be free.

Sandra: And where do you feel it in your body when you say I want to be free?

Sue: It's fear, in my chest.

We soften and release the energy in the same way; it flows up and out of her mouth. The dialogue continues in this way releasing the energy related to various thoughts about her husband, until we touch on the intimacy issues.

Sandra: So, how attracted are you to your husband?

Sue: Well I don't really fancy him any more, say a 6 out of 10.

Sandra: So when you think about what you don't fancy, where do you feel it in your body?

Sue: In my heart.

We soften and release it.

Sue: Well, actually, I do love him. I can see me looking forward to him coming home from work, but then when he gets home and is actually there and he starts to approach me physically I feel blocked about it. It's out there (points in front of her) a block between us.

Sandra guides Sue to soften this energy, which Sue indicated was outside her body.

Sue: It's melted and is on the floor. Oh, it's coming in through my feet and up my body, and out through my mouth.

Sandra: Ok let it flow up and out and tell me when it's all cleared through.

Sue: It's clear.

Sandra: Ok. Now, your husband comes home from work; you're looking forward to seeing him. You know he'll want to be intimate with you. How do you feel?

Sue: Smiles...God, this is amazing!

Sandra: When was the last time you felt this way towards your husband?

Sue: A couple of years ago!

The couple have restored their intimate relationship and are now making plans to move back together again.

The story, "His Stress Was Too Much For Me," of Amy and John on page 165, is a similar story with a happy ending for your inspiration. These stories are real, and this is exactly how the sessions went. I have related the detail to show you how easy it is and how so many relationships fail unnecessarily. Many people I work with tell me how they wish they knew how to do this before they got divorced, to have given themselves a chance.

Separation and Life after Divorce

For some of us, separation is the right thing. Maybe we actually came together for the wrong reasons; e.g. being so young without knowing who we are yet. And as we grow and discover more about ourselves, we know we want something else for ourselves (*see* "After the Affair," page 173).

For others, the damage is too much to repair without help and we didn't have this knowledge when we needed it. Now we just have to get through as best we can and get on with a new life. EmoTrance can help us do that. Janet is an example of how you can get through and how big a difference the right knowledge and tools can be.

Whatever the reasons, divorce means big changes and a lot of different and new challenges to deal with: where to live, finances, children and work. That's a lot for any human being to handle, which means we will feel all kinds of emotions in the process.

But we know that all these negative emotions are arising from the build up of energy as our spiritual body handles it all, and that we can pay it some attention, feel the pain and help keep the flow going. We also know that all life experiences, when we do allow ourselves to experience them fully and then let go, can bring us an enormous amount of strength and wisdom.

Here is Janet's story:

Surviving to Thriving after Divorce

My very first experience of EmoTrance was a one-day workshop with Sandra Hillawi—the first of a two-day Practitioner's Course. It was a brilliant summer's day, blue sky, fluffy white clouds and our small group were gathered at a beautiful country house near Bath.

But my heart was far from sunny. A black cloud of fear and sadness hung over me as my relationship with my partner was under strain and I knew he wanted to split up and sell our home. This was a great worry to me, because when my ex-husband had remarried he'd stopped supporting my son, who was at drama school, and due to the stress I'd been under, my business wasn't doing very well either. I was really scared that on my own I'd never be able to afford to get a new home for my son and me and support him through the rest of his course.

I knew deep down that my fear and negativity were very counter-productive and that I should try to overcome them, but however hard I tried nothing was working. So when we started practising EmoTrance on one another, I plucked up the courage to confide in my partner and work on the problem with her.

As we sat on a wooden bench in the shade of a small tree, she gently encouraged me to connect with my feelings of fear and insecurity. I took some deep breaths and concentrated on the process of releasing. I was amazed at how quickly I felt calmer and how soon I found myself much more relaxed about the situation, even though in reality, my circumstances had not changed. It was almost unbelievable and I wondered whether it would hold.

I need not have worried. The very next day I received a letter from my partner's solicitor confirming my worst fears. I opened it while we were having breakfast together and casually tossed it onto the table with the calm remark, "Oh, so that's why you've been acting so strangely lately." My reaction shocked me—but nothing like how much it shocked my partner!

Over the following years I have continued to use EmoTrance on myself and it has pulled me through every challenge I encountered: my break up, house move, supporting my son through his course, making a new home for us and re-building my business in another town.

I have also had the joy of sharing its gentle power with my clients and helping them overcome fears and phobias, break through depression, transform poor relationships, enhance self esteem and beat emotional eating disorders.

Earlier this year I also trained as an EmoTrance Trainer.

I believe that with EmoTrance, whatever your problem is, if you can bear to feel it, you can heal it.

↬

Please use Exercise 6: Letting Go of the Painful Past (page 37), to help you through a life transition from Separation to Divorce.

CHAPTER 22

It's Tearing Me Apart: Ending Conflicts

*C*onflict between different aspects of our lives can cause procrastination, inaction and inertia, and is a form of blocked energy that can stop what we want from really manifesting for us.

Common conflicts people have are:

- Work and Relationships

- Work and Family

- Work and Motherhood

- Can't Live with Her; Can't Live Without Her

- Need to be Free, but Can't Let Go

- Love and Money

Each side of the conflict is in itself a complex energetic entity or thought field, a concept made up of lots of emotions, beliefs and experiences. We learned how we can manipulate these energies and change our concepts earlier, but now we are looking at the relationship between two concepts.

Resolving conflicts by transforming the energy of the conflict is so simple and quick to do, allowing change or requiring clarity. The Rainbow Technique is a great way to help change the energetics of conflicting concepts.

When I resolved my conflict between Work and Relationships a couple of years ago, a conflict that had consequences in my life that I was living out; namely, that while work was flowing well I didn't actually have a relationship in my life. Once resolved, the following month, he arrived!

A simple way is to think of both sides of the conflict at the same time, then feel in your body where that conflict is held. Soften, flow and release; repeat until you feel clear.

If each concept seems very disconnected or very far removed from each other, you can use Exercise 10: Conflict Resolution—The Rainbow Technique (page 74).

Conflict Resolution—The Rainbow Technique

Contemplate what conflicts you are facing right now. Take each part of the concept one by one.

Ask yourself to contemplate for a moment the first concept. Point out in space where you feel that concept resides. Now do the same for the opposite side of the conflict. Where does this concept reside?

Now quite possibly you have a sense of two thought fields out there, probably disconnected.

First of all just ask: "Do these concepts positions need to be adjusted first?" If so, allow them to move in space till it feels more comfortable to you.

What we want to do is connect those energies together.

Using your hand and moving it in space from one concept to the other, take the energy from one side in a semi-circle up and over to the other concept connecting them both. Then continue with your hand to take the energy from this concept downwards completing the circle back to the first concept. You will feel a difference already in the energy. Let these energies run in this circular path more quickly. You do this by just thinking that it's happening.

Diagram 6 Resolving conflicts involving money and love with the Rainbow Connection.

Now contemplate both concepts together. Is the conflict still there?

What does it mean in your life that this conflict has now resolved?

For some it will feel right that the energy of the two connected concepts or thought fields needs to flow in to us and out again. If so, again, just have this intention for the energy to flow in, soften and flow as it comes in, let it flow back out to the thought field in front of you and again contemplate how that feels and what that means now for you. Can you see a way forward?

CHAPTER 23

The Law of Attraction

M any people have experimented with the Law of Attraction, as revealed in *The Secret*,[10] to attract the things they want into their life. The Law states that you attract what you focus on, but that our negative emotions and limiting beliefs can stop us attracting what we want, as these are energy blockages disrupt the flow. We can use our new skills in transforming emotional energy to make the Law of Attraction work better for us in manifesting or attracting into our lives what we want.

Making the Law of Attraction Work For You

By building a concept of what you do want, you are creating a thought field. By focusing upon that daily, you are making a dense thought field. By checking out your relationship with the concept you have created, you can identify and clear the energetic resistance (negative emotions and limiting beliefs) to that concept that are manifesting, by noting where you feel that, then softening and flowing. By inviting in the energy of your concept that you have created, and letting it flow through you, and clearing any disturbances along the way, you create the positive emotional flow states of 'already having your target' in your life. You now radiate this energy flow state, which is the 'attractor factor.'

Attracting the Partner You Want

For all the single people out there, this is exciting and also a very interesting self exploration creating the energetic flow and states to enable this to happen. For those who are in a relationship, this still applies. You have the possibility of having and developing what you want.

Here we will be using the Law of Attraction. To get what you want, you have to first know what you want, become what you want—in other words, feel that you already have it!

For example, to have someone who loves and adores you, learn how to love and adore yourself, then he/she will show up more easily because you have created the flow path for this energy in your life. If you have an energy disturbance inside; e.g., if you are feeling right now that "I don't love myself," ask yourself where do I feel that? Maybe it's in your heart, maybe your solar plexus. Either way, it's an energy disturbance, an interruption in the flow required to attract love into your life. You may actually have someone around who loves or admires you, but your blocked energy may be stopping the moments or opportunities from taking place that will allow that potential to actualise and blossom.

Personally, the things I did to meet my soul mate were:

ॐ Dropping my shields to learn to reconnect with love and life

ॐ Heart healing and learning to love myself

ॐ Discovering what I wanted!

ॐ Resolving conflicts; in my case work and relationships

Then the energy pathway was there for the right man to arrive. Past relationships, which were unsuccessful, mirrored my previous energetic patterns. For example, while I was shielded and disconnected, I attracted and pursued the macho male type, strong protective energy. My emotional neediness, arising from the deficiency I was in, became a problem when the attentiveness was not so regular. Also, the same tough demeanour meant that this kind of guy wasn't comfortable dealing with emotions at all. So I was attracting something that matched where I was at. There was a kind of love, a kind of flow, but with all kinds of pain also. It just didn't work out.

When I became open, connected, with strong heart energy and the energy pathways were clear to attract a warm open-hearted man, that's what I attracted. A man who had the same capacity to handle life, to handle me and my emotional states, to be open and honest and courageous enough to be able to experience love so deeply himself. And I didn't even believe that kind of man existed before! He was out there, but until I changed my energetics I couldn't find the love that I wanted.

The exact steps that you need to take may be quite different from mine as we are each starting from our own unique place according to our past experiences and how we handled that so far. My own experiences illustrate the principles at work and can give you some inspiration to find your own direction and areas to change.

Here's an inspiring story of Joan, and her success attracting the man she wanted using the Law of Attraction and EmoTrance.

Joan was Ready for a New Romance

How we helped Joan get through her bereavement when she lost her husband to cancer, is the subject of another story. A lot of it took place in a coffee shop where we met, after one of her last visits to the hospital. We cleared a lot of the intense emotions, which were coming from great sadness in her chest and head. We even looked ahead to the inevitable, and cleared a lot of energy in advance, which enabled her to ride the wave of his passing and the subsequent events with grace and greater strength of heart. Suffice to say that the time came when this bright over 50-year-old friend of mine was thinking about finding a new relationship. She'd signed on a dating website, but so far hadn't met anyone that sparked her interest.

We decided to explore, making this more energetically possible. In actual fact she said she would like to meet her soul mate. I asked her to start to imagine out there somewhere what a soul mate is, all that he would be, the qualities she was looking for, any practical requirements, and to allow an image or sense of who that was to form in front of her. We were building a thought field composed of everything she wanted.

Using Exercise 11: Attracting the Partner You Want (page 78), I asked her now to make a connection to this thought field of her soul mate and check out what she felt in her body. There was instant fear and complex reactions going on in her body. In the usual EmoTrance way we softened and flowed and we cleared them all.

Then I directed her to invite this energy in, through and out. Well, there were all kinds of resistance. It took about half an hour to release all the issues, manifesting as energy disturbances in various places, a lot of yawning and a lot of upward wind, and finally we got it all flowing. She said it felt really good; it felt like she had it—like he was here. She was totally ready and excited now, a long way from the apprehensive, anxious Joan we started with earlier.

Some time after that, she encountered and met a new friend, John, and everything was going really well. She called me to say how he had everything she had asked for and she was very happy as they shared many interests. After a few months, her new friend was called away on a family crisis suddenly leaving her quite bereft. We had a lot of softening and flowing to do for the pain of loss, as she'd really allowed herself to open up to this man and felt deeply hurt about the sudden loss and the way he had made no contact for so long. We got her through that. She returned to being her happy self. When he finally came back on the scene a couple of months later, she discovered how difficult it was for him to communicate and express his emotions, when it came down to real issues. Realising that this was something important to her, she decided that maybe he wasn't everything she wanted. So we started again.

This time Joan built a picture of everything she wanted before, but in addition she wanted the ability to communicate on an emotional level, and while she was at it, someone who could help her with the computer would also be useful! The Law of Attraction is a great powerful force. Being able to transform your own energy system to harness the power of the Law of Attraction is great fun very rewarding and amazing when it happens. This time Joan worked on her own energy, softening and flowing this new concept that she had built, in, through and out, clearing all resistances until she felt all the feelings and energy states as if she had it already. She checked into that energy periodically to remind herself of it, but went about her life. She met her next

Attracting the Partner You Want

You can do this alone or have a friend assist you. Bear in mind this process can work for attracting other things that you may want in your life too.

Build the Vision of What You Want

Visualise an image of what you want. Allow that to become more detailed with all the attributes of a person you would hope for, maybe physical, emotional, qualities, practical requirements and shared interests.

Check the Position of the Thought Field

Ask yourself: is this vision located in the right place or does it feel like it needs to move in space so it sits more comfortably? If so, allow it to move appropriately.

Connect with the Vision

Reach out your heart sensors and connect with this thought field. Notice what happens in your body. Clear any disturbances using EmoTrance until you feel ready to invite the energy in.

Invite the Energy In, Through and Out

As you invite the energy in you may feel strong sensations in the body. Soften, flow and release these energies. Continue to bring the vision energy in, through and out. As it flows out, let it flow back to your original vision, brightening and feeding that vision. Again, invite the Vision energy in, through and out. Create a strong circle of energy flow, breathing it all in. Have the intention the energy flows faster until you feel great about your Vision.

Examine Your Energy and Emotional State

You are aiming to feel all the feelings and all the energies of what you are aiming to attract. Anything less, locate the problem, soften and flow, until you are there. You will know when you are there, because it will feel so good and it will feel like you actually have that already.

Reconnect Periodically

At regular intervals, reconnect with your vision energy and repeat the process. This will keep your energy system in the states of flow to attract this in your life.

Other Approaches

Write a list of what you want and go through a similar energetic process. If you already have a partner and you do these exercises, don't be surprised if the energy dynamics start to change in your existing relationship. You might already be with the one you really want, but you just couldn't see that.

When we are transforming emotional energy with EmoTrance, all we need do is identify the location of the energy and work with that energy to restore the flow. We do not have to know the psychological aspects of that energy, although we often get insights as we access and start to release those energies. If we do, it's interesting, but incidental, as in a few moments, that issue will be gone anyway.

man friend, Malcolm, at a dancing class. He was every bit the gentleman and all of the fun of the last man friend, but this time, was more emotionally mature and guess what? He was a computer programmer! They are very happy and the relationship is progressing beautifully.

To get the Law of Attraction working for you depends on you knowing what you want, clearing all your resistances to the actuality of what you want, having the energy state and feelings as if you already have it, to create a free path of energy flow from the universe to and through you, then allowing what you want to attract to turn up.

CHAPTER 24

Allowing Yourself to Fall in Love

This subject is a most wonderful one to talk about, and even better to experience. Many of us have been in love, are in love and some of us maybe haven't had that experience—ever. For some it was a slow process, for others it happened so fast. For me, it was fast, but understanding energy dynamics made a big difference. Sometimes the principles are best illustrated by stories, so I will share a couple of mine since I was conscious of the energy processes at work at the time.

You know the expression, "the way to a man's heart is through his stomach," in other words, feed him? Well the food we are talking about is energy nutrition.

I went on holiday in December 2004. It was my first holiday for ages and I decided to make it a playground for exploring energy while I was there. My first opportunity was actually on day one, on the glass bottomed boat, where I drew in the energies of the stunning blue sea, the corals and the colourful fish. Tears of joy and delight streamed down my face and thrilled my body as I soaked in and flowed those energies through. Wow! It was a great start to the holiday!

The local people were very friendly open-hearted people—and they were very forward. Some were after tips, some after my custom, some after my body, or a visa, and some were just friendly and polite, wanting to make friends and connections or to help.

I went with a friend. Our energy systems were very, very different. If somebody approached me to talk or invite me to look at anything, I met them with an open heart, a radiant smile (I was happy) and I gave them my full attention. I listened, accepted what they had to say, sometimes accepted their offer to come in their shop for tea and a browse, and sometimes I just thanked them, spoke some words of appreciation, and declined. But I took the time to interact, to get to know people, and all my interactions were open hearted, accepting and sincere, with some kind of appreciation and thanks in return, whether it was the door man, the merchant, the driver, the excursion rep, the manager or the waiter. I found it interesting to observe how enjoyable those interactions were when I took the time to make them. Our lives are so busy that often we just don't allow the time to connect with others properly.

Meanwhile, my friend was very distressed saying, "No, no I'm not interested, go away!" She was totally closed and felt under pressure that they were all so pushy. Basically, she had a completely different experience to me on the same holiday. She hated it; I loved it. My experience was wonderful. A whole week of heart-warming interactions with warm friendly human beings, taking the time to pay them attention, to listen, accept, recognise and appreciate them with a smile and heartfelt words of thanks. Whatever anyone's original intentions were, their intentions were transformed by my energy dynamics. The result was that I was treated like a queen with total respect and adoration. By the end of the week there were five men standing by the bus, all in love, waving me off as I went off to the airport.

Falling in Love Ingredients

We all need attention, acceptance, recognition and appreciation. These are essential energy nutrients. Sometimes, while getting to know someone, we can be more focussed on getting and enjoying these things that we need. We will like anyone who gives us these energies as it makes us feel good. If we keep getting more of the same, and we keep feeling good, we could easily allow ourselves to fall in love with that person; i.e. we let their energy in completely and our resistances literally fall away. So we can also turn that around and become aware of what people need and give them what they need. Try giving these energies to others and see how they fall for you. As we have seen earlier, some people will have resistance to this kind of attention no matter how sincere, because of their past experience, but remember what comes from the heart goes directly and most easily into the heart of another.

What we see physically; i.e. appearance is also an energy that we take in. So physical beauty also affects us; we take that energy in, we feel it. It feels so good we want more of it. We are attracted to it. We take it in more and more and we can fall in love with what we see as the energy of physical beauty. If the energy of the person within is also radiant, the combination can be 'irresistible;' we are taking that energy in more and more. Our resistances 'fall away' creating a strong and very wonderful flow state within, which we call 'being in love.' The trouble is, if we fall in love with only physical beauty and then when we get to the know the person, we may find that the flow gets interrupted and life with them is a bit more challenging! But then, we know how to restore the flow now!

But this book is not so much about physical beauty, but the beauty of the spirit within, how to make that radiant and so shiny that beauty radiates brightly from the inside, and how to create such flow within that we are radiant and confident, which is an attractive energy. (More of that later.) Here's another illustration, my own falling in love experience.

When Sandra Met Khaled

Let's start at the beginning. In June 2005, I met a man online who was to become my beautiful husband. The previous month I had done some work on the energy of relationships in my life and releasing the conflict I had between work and relationships. I was out with a girlfriend that evening sitting at the Quays in Portsmouth overlooking the harbour, and as you do, eyeing up the guys sitting out on the terrace. It struck me how there were none whose energy I resonated with or found attractive. I found that curious, but dismissed it. Later that evening we went up to the Middle Eastern Restaurant and the manager walked out to serve us. He was not physically what I would normally find attractive, but I was struck immediately by his energy. It was the heart energy; there was warmth and openness. I liked him immediately and for the first time I recognised what it was that I wanted: that heart energy in my man. Sadly that degree of heart openness and warmth was missing in British culture. As a culture we are more closed and guarded and take longer to open up and accept people. Men especially struggle with that openness, as openness means they often feel uncomfortable with their emotions. So it was the strong warm courageous heart energy, that I wanted. For the first time I actually knew what I was looking for. And where had I met that before in abundance? On holiday in Egypt.

That night I was pottering about on my laptop, and having had that insight I was trying to connect with the Egyptian energy. So I was just browsing around Egyptian themes with no particular aim but to recall the places I'd been to and the people I'd met and I saw a name that resonated exactly with my insight. I sent a "Hi" message and the next day we started to chat.

So there we were—me in the UK and him in Cairo chatting online with our web cameras, getting to know each other. He was interesting: a businessman, divorced, intelligent and seemed nice but…I was being cagey, cautious and very cool. After all, there wasn't any real point in making an effort—he was in another country, so the relationship was a non-starter, even if he was interested in me and seemed to be very warm and sincere man.

After a while I began to be aware of my blocking behaviour and thought, "What am I doing? Here I am, a teacher of energy flow in health and relationships, and I'm consciously resisting and blocking this energy coming my way. And he seems like a nice guy." So it began, initially, as an interesting experiment. "Let's see what would happen if I applied EmoTrance techniques and principles every step of the way in a brand new relationship." So I started to soften and flow my resistances. For example, he would compliment me, and my initial response was "hmmm yeah; sure he means it, I'm not falling for that one," so where did I feel that? That was a pressure in my chest…focus, soften, flow and release then I could accept the compliment and actually feel nice about it, and say "thank you," as actually it was really sweet. So it continued, my fears and my beliefs; e.g. "It's never gonna work; he's in Egypt for God's sake!"—that was in my stomach—soften and flow. So when I received more appreciation from him, being able to accept it made me feel really good and all I did was say "thanks" and "that was really nice of you to say that." As I started to open up, and become more interested in him, up came the "whoa, but I don't want to fall in love; I might get hurt again!" Again, where did I feel that? In my heart—soften and flow.

So the weeks went on. We chatted and got to know each other. I accepted whatever energies he sent, said thanks and offered recognition and appreciation in return following the principle: energy needs to flow and everyone needs energy nutrition. So what happened? For him, here was a woman giving him complete acceptance and real appreciation of who he was and what he said, which was so rare to find and totally irresistible—literally, he couldn't resist! He had absolutely no choice but to fall in love with me; i.e. he completely let me in, opened his heart and received all my attention and appreciation deeply, and felt wonderful.

Then, everything intensified. From his strong flow state, he started to send me such amazing and wonderful feelings and expressions from his heart. It was pouring out. My response? "Whooaahh!! Slow down; I can't handle that!" Hmmm, that was interesting; I was holding it back again. I am holding back love. So, I thought why am I doing that? Breathe, soften, flow—accepted the energy. It was a lot, but boy was it beautiful to accept when I could handle it. It was warmth like flowing honey through my whole body. Wow! Amazing! So, naturally, I was falling in love in return. I now had complete openness and was letting him and all his feelings towards me in. And that's how we started! Three months from our first chat I booked my flight to Cairo to meet this man I had fallen for at the beautiful Zamelek Palace, Marriott Hotel on the Nile. It was a romantic, exotic adventure; a wonderful week I will never forget and before it ended I knew without a doubt that my heart had found its home at last. Was there any fear whatsoever? No. Not a single iota. I smile as I imagine your own energy systems churning now as you read this and my response to you is this... Where do you feel that in your body? Breathe into it, let it soften and flow!

Incidentally, I discovered later that he had only joined the Egyptian site the day before I found him, and I was the first person to connect with him. Was that a miracle? Divine intervention? Synchronicity? Or the Law of Attraction at work?

I will some share more aspects of the energy dynamics of this relationship later. But the message is: energy needs to flow and everyone needs energy nutrition. That's the principle I was living out, and that I continue to live out and which has brought us deep happiness and love, despite the great challenges of our circumstances, the challenges themselves being handled in the same way, by transforming the emotional energy.

So falling in love: It depends on you opening your heart enough to let another person and their energy in. The more open and the more you can accept to flow in and through, the easier and quicker you will fall in love. So why all this caution? Where do you feel that fear in your body? Soften and flow. Live, enjoy, be happy!

So Could You Fall in Love with Anyone?

Yes. It doesn't mean that you lose your mind, or that you are unable to think and know what you want. But it's a choice. You allow yourself to be open and to allow someone in. The energy does the rest of the magic. But remember also, the opportunities that come your way are the result of what you are attracting by the state of your energy system. We have already explored about how to attract what you want, and how to be what you want so that the universe can let it flow your way. Later we will explore how to love yourself more and attract even more love. But even when opportunity knocks on the door, you still have to open it and let it in. For all the preparation I did leading up to this, I could have said no at any point for any of the reasons I shared with you, but then I never would have had the experience that came with the yes —and that's always your free choice.

A Long Engagement?

When my client Beverley told me she was engaged for four years I was astonished.

"Four years? Why haven't you got married yet?" I asked her.

"Oh well, I love him very much, but I'm just waiting until I can be totally sure."

"What's holding you back?"

"I keep hearing my mum's voice in my head saying, 'you can never trust a man completely'. She had a bad time with my dad playing away."

I asked her to think about her mum's experience of her husband having an affair, and where did she feel that? It was in her chest. We released it. Then I asked her that because that happened to her mum, how much did she believe it could happen to her, on a scale of 0–10? She said 4.

So I asked the usual question, "Where do you feel that in your body?"

"In my head," she replied.

We released it. Then I asked her about her mum's words: "You can never trust a man completely." We discovered she felt that in her chest also; we released it. Beverley was now starting to feel really happy and excited and free.

"What's stopping you from getting married now?" I asked.

"Nothing," she replied, laughing. "He's completely different from all those guys. He treats me so well, and I do love him and he loves me so much. I can't believe I've resisted it for so long. That's amazing!"

Being so Open is Risky; What if it Goes Wrong?

If you don't know how to transform emotional energy, then yes, you might feel hurt. But not if you have read this book and are starting to apply these principles in your life. Fear of being hurt, fear of being seen, fear of being rejected are all just energy blockages in the path that stop the flow, and so stop us actually experiencing love. It's all energy. If it hurts, the energy just got stuck, so breathe, soften and flow. A few minutes later you're through it. So why hold back life for the sake of a few moments of pain that can be gone so easily in literally moments and transform and enrich us along the way?

EmoTrance means you can release the fear. It's now safe to open up, fall in love, live to the max, enjoy life. And if it goes wrong or you break up down the line, you can repair any energetic injuries easily, and you will have had some great times along the way. Chances are, that by applying these energy principles through the relationship, you will have more chance of lasting success in that relationship. By continuing to clear the little things and even handle the big things as they occur in relationships, you can maintain a state of clear connection and love. It's the fact that we don't process, learn and let go, and we don't have the ability to handle the big stuff that causes our relationships to fail.

CHAPTER 25

Curing A Crush

Let's consider another type of falling in love. A crush is an obsession with another person who has triggered previously unknown feelings, thoughts and sensations and is essentially synonymous with falling in love.

A crush can happen to anyone, at any time; it can involve a film star, a neighbour, a total stranger on a train and it matters absolutely not one iota whether this person—the object of attraction—is aware of this or interested in any aspect of it *at all*.

Silvia Hartmann shared her insights on Crushes with me and how to deal with them in this chapter.

Structurally, something happens inside the person who is experiencing the crush; it completely belongs to that person and it is, in fact, the first time a new kind of circuitry is fired off or comes online inside the person who experiences the crush. It's like the lights on a Christmas Tree coming on because someone accidentally touched a loose bulb.

Now that may sound utterly unromantic, and you're right, it is. It is a structural thing that happens to people and if only it was handled correctly, could herald a whole new dawn of wonderful understandings, feelings, a different kind of life filled to the brim with love, joy and happiness…

But that's not the experience of people who have fallen prey to a crush. They are first of all, totally confused by the enormity of the emotions they are experiencing, probably for the very first time ever.

Secondly, they are distracted from these internal experiences by their external obsession to the person who triggered the crush. Because the immense swoop of feelings happened because of that person, the owner of the crush can't help but tie the two together, like this:

"I feel such amazing emotions I've never felt before when I see Pete. That means it is Pete who makes these emotions—Pete makes me feel this way."

Pete becomes the creator of good feelings, the cause, the reason and thus, the total focus of attention for the crushed. Now, it's all about Pete. The more we can look at Pete, the better we feel; if we can't look at Pete, we feel terrible. Each and every aspect of this in practise strengthens the idea that it is Pete who is in charge here;

that it is Pete who is the solution to the problem, the remedy for the pain, the bringer of joy and everything else besides.

Pete, in the meantime, may be on the other side of the planet, utterly oblivious, otherwise engaged, or just simply not interested at all.

To outside observers, such as friends, family and the parents of teenage daughters, as well as therapists, it is obvious that this isn't about Pete, because Pete plays no part in this drama other than his mere existence, for which he cannot be held responsible.

To the person on the inside of the crush, this is not only *not* obvious, but completely unbelievable. They have structurally and neurologically tied the feelings to the object of attraction, by virtue of design, by reflex, because that is how people work.

How to Help a Friend Get Over a Crush

So the very first step for anyone who wants to help another get over a crush in a healthy manner and learn the right lessons from this extraordinary occurrence is to understand that, for a person inside of a crush situation, it is an absolute reality that Pete, the object of attraction, is what is making all of this happen.

Please understand that you cannot tell a person under the spell of a crush that they are wrong; that Pete doesn't care, that this "isn't real" (because for them, it really doesn't get any more real than this, believe you me!).

You cannot argue with a person under the spell of a crush. You can't use ordinary logic or reason with them. Any kind of counter-evidence doesn't stand up to the sheer force of the emotional experiences the person is going through. What we can do, however, is to listen. That is the first start.

"When you think about Pete, what do you feel? Where do you feel this?"

In these simple questions, there lie many magic seeds for helping the crushed person through the transition they are making—from someone who has no idea what love feels like, to someone who recognises it, understands it, welcomes it and is able to interact with others on a whole new level altogether.

Falling in love is an enlightenment experience. A crush is an enlightenment experience.

Don't denigrate it; don't say, "He or she will get over it."

That's not enough. Most people come out of first loves and crushes so terribly damaged and disappointed, so disheartened and in so much pain, that they make decisions about love which will haunt them possibly forever and may destroy entire incarnations in the process.

That's a terrible thing, a terrible price to pay. It is important that we should learn to treasure crushes and make sure that the person comes out on the other side strengthened, wiser and healthy and whole, ready to love again, and again, and again, deeper, more profoundly, and with more wisdom and experience each time it presents itself.

"When you think about Pete, what do you feel? Where do you feel this?"

In this sentence, we start out from where the person is—constantly thinking outwards, towards Pete. That is the direction of their attention, they can't help it, that is how it works.

"When you think about Pete…" aligns us with the reality of that person. We are on their side, not trying to talk them out of it, or change the direction of their attention at this time. The next part of the sentence goes on and follows the same route that happens naturally in the person, namely their response to the original object of attraction—how Pete makes them feel.

"When you think about Pete, what do you feel?"

Now, the attention is on the feelings—it has actually been withdrawn from Pete and placed back where it belongs, inside the person themselves. That's the power place, the power point, even if people don't know this.

The fact is that Pete can't help us at all, even if he is willing. Pete is on the outside. The way the person feels can't be changed from the outside, even though it may appear that way; the way person feels must be changed by the person, from the inside.

"What do you feel?" does that. It takes the person to where the real power resides, namely inside their own body.

We go on to specify the question, not by asking for a bunch of labels such as "depressed–hopeless–overwhelmed–miserable–angry," and not for asking for a bunch of metaphors like "my heart is blossoming like a lotus flower; my soul is singing like a bird; I am drowning in a purple ocean of love."

We are asking, "What do you feel? Where do you feel this?"

We are trying to get a factual description of the physical symptoms of having fallen prey to crush, or having fallen in love, if that term is preferred. We are looking for terms that are direct and describe directly a physical sensation, such as:

"I feel a hot burning in my chest."

"My stomach is all in knots and I can't breathe."

"My head feels like it's going to explode with the pressure."

Theoretically, when a person "falls in love," there should be a clean lightning strike of energy that runs through all their systems in an instant leaving them delighted, smiling, refreshed, very proactive, very logical and present and correct.

All the "love pain" that people experience is only due to the fact that people's love circuitry is not functioning as it should. There are places in the energy body that are incapable of handling the lightning strike energy and it is there where things get stuck and hit existing injuries and blockages. When they do, it actually hurts.

That's where love hurts.

The physical sensations of pain in the heart, pressure in the chest and stomach, which can be literally unbearably painful, are not given enough credence and attention when people try to help others who are suffering from the effects of a crush.

The helpers think it's all in the head, but it isn't. If it was, it would be easy to overcome; the very reason that crushes and falling in love with the wrong person is such a problem is exactly because it is so very physical in all its manifestations.

And that is also exactly how a crushed person knows that this is absolutely real.

And they're right! It is absolutely real. Now, we have asked the question.

"When you think about Pete, what do you feel? Where do you feel this?"

Let's imagine that we've asked a lady friend of ours, who is sitting on her bed in her room, in floods of tears "because of Pete."

Now, we need to listen to what she says. We need to watch her very carefully. As she is crying, her hands may be before her eyes. When we ask the question, her hands move from her eyes to her chest perhaps, holding on to herself, showing us directly where the worst pain resides.

Let's keep it going. "Does it hurt where your heart is?"

Ask. Don't tell her what she should or should not be feeling, thinking, doing. Work with what is right there.

"What are you feeling?"

She tells us things and we listen with our ears, but we also listen with our eyes. Watch very carefully what gestures she makes, how she moves her body as she tells us and shows us her pain, her injury.

We can now say, "Look, there's something wrong with your heart. Not with your beating heart, but with your heart of energy and that's why it hurts so much. Love is a good thing, it should feel good. Shall we try and heal your heart?"

Please note that we are not offering to "get rid of Pete" or in any way to exorcise their affection for the object of attraction. That will all happen wonderfully and naturally once the poor person's energy system has been restored to full functioning. They won't be in excruciating pain any longer and they'll be able to think for themselves again and make rational decisions.

Personally, I have never met a person in terrible pain who would not welcome the idea of alleviating that pain somewhat, even just a little bit.

However, should any objections occur, you can always point out that a fully functioning heart of energy works much better—you get to love Pete even more than you already do. This is about you, not about Pete. Don't you want to be the best you can possibly be?

In all reality, there is never a reason to not be healed in energy work. Every person has inside themselves not just a drive towards health and what we call "The

Even Flow," but also an understanding and recognition of when things are right and when they are wrong.

Everyone, even a small child, understands innately that if you are broken, you are not going to get what you want, whatever that may be, but if you are repaired, you have a much better chance. It is this innate and incontrovertible understanding which convinces people to do the structural repair work of simply "putting to rights what once went wrong," as the saying goes in EmoTrance.

It is an essential movement away from pain and towards pleasure, which is the most basic wiring of any living thing. When you call upon this in EmoTrance, objections melt away and people become ready to at least attempt a healing.

Once our person has agreed that to attempt to heal the heart is a good idea, we can say, "Put your hands on your heart. Send all the healing energy you have to your heart; whatever you have to give. I'm going to do the same thing. You work from the inside, I work from the outside and between the two of us, let's see if we can't make this better…Let's find out if we can make you feel better."

EmoTrance is a wonderfully loving thing. It is beautiful in how unconditional this is.

Our ladyfriend doesn't have to "give up" anything. She doesn't have to first vow to not love Pete anymore. She doesn't have to explain herself. She doesn't have to admit to having been "wrong" to fall in love with him in the first place.

We are here to pay attention to her alone and to help her feel better. That's all. That is exquisite, beautiful and extraordinary. It gives the power back to the person who is receiving this kind of unconditional support from the other (you!); it leaves all choices and decisions with her after the healing is completed. It supports her and her alone.

If you, as the helper in this situation, can enter into "the spirit of EmoTrance" and allow yourself also to forget all about Pete and simply focus on healing the person in front of you, with all your heart, you will be surprised how open and ready the other becomes to receive your support and take the energy you are offering to make it a part of their healing process. Even teenagers with their parents, if approached in that way, will allow that sort of unconditional support to enter into them and help them through a crush crisis.

There is more to this than meets the eye at first glance.

Any movement of energy during even a half-hearted, first attempt in the experience of the physical pain is, for the person who is feeling all of this, akin to a revelation. Any movement will give them hope—"Oh my God, I really can do something to help myself in this experience of suffering! There is movement, I'm not stuck anymore!"

EmoTrance is something that is essentially designed to be a life skill, something that once it has been experienced, once it has been learned, will and can come to the rescue from that moment forth and will literally transform the experience of a person.

With crushes and being in love, there are huge waves of emotions involved. There are huge physical sensations that can strike at any time, that can involve literally every part of the body.

Just the thought alone that "This is only an energy!" is a saving grace. Before, how would you explain how you feel to yourself? What was going on with you? How was this caused and how to alleviate it? There was total helplessness, overwhelming and non-understanding, plus the very real fear that one might be going out of control, going insane and the further repercussions of those sort of thoughts on a person's behaviour after the fact.

A little heart healing later and… "When you think about Pete, what do you feel? Where do you feel this in your body?"

(Deep, deep sigh of relief): "I feel…lighter, so much better…(sighs again deeply)…Now, I feel like a pressure in my (…)"

"That too, is only an energy. You've done so well! Just let that flow away as well…and keep breathing deeply."

That is something so simple and so easy that anyone can learn to do it, learn to facilitate it. Yes, you, whoever you are, you can use this when your friends and relatives are struck by the spell of the crush.

You can use this for yourself, by yourself, or you can tell a friend about it and you can do it together.

"Love Pain" can be healed and cured—only if you work directly with the energy system. But when you do, it is extraordinary how gentle, easy and profound the healing becomes and how much better we can all start to feel as a result and right away.

There is no need to die of a broken heart any longer; there is no need to try and live for years with the pain of love, obsession, misery after failed affairs, break ups and unrequited crushes. There is no need any longer to get to age 87 and still declare that the "only person I ever loved broke my heart when I was 14 and I have never loved again."

EmoTrance gives us an incredibly easy way to cure love pain and to open up the doors to a life full of love, love that delights, not hurts; love that gives us wings, not diseases.

It's as simple as that, really. Try it.

Try it with real people, in real life situations, when you can see, hear and feel they are suffering. You don't have to be a therapist, or a healer. Any human being can help another using these simple words, this simple system and that's what it was always designed to do.

Let your love flow freely and may it always be joyous.

CHAPTER 26

*F*eeding Your Love

I feel I only repeat myself again here. The recipe is the same. Energy needs to flow and everyone needs Energy Nutrition. Keep living this principle in your relationship and your relationship will grow.

But there is one additional phenomenon to understand when you look at the dynamic of two people's energy systems working together.

Energy Needs to Flow means everyone needs to feel accepted—whatever emotional state they may be coming from.

What happens is this: The person doing the accepting is a release path for the built up energy of the person who maybe feeling stressed.

Everyone Needs Energy Nutrition means we all need attention; recognition of who we are, how we are feeling, what we do and appreciation of that. Having had their energy accepted, then receiving a soothing recognition and appreciation in return is wonderful way of restoring flow for both and deepening the relationship.

As you live your relationship with this dynamic, what happens is each partner learns at a more deeper level who the other is. "I've got you under my skin," sang Frank Sinatra. Literally, we are taking in the energy of the other person on a daily basis, and they taking you in. As that flows through and out, it changes us; it becomes part of us. You come to know each other deeply. Intimacy grows. The deeper and the stronger the flow, the deeper the love.

As you consciously take the time to pay attention, to recognise and to appreciate and to show your love in various ways, you are feeding your partner 'energy nutrients' and creating a stronger heart energy and a stronger energy flow in them, which in turn radiates back to you.

Couples in successful long-term relationships often say one of their secrets is "never going to bed on an argument." What they are doing is: one is paying attention to the other and listening, allowing the other to get everything off their chest. Really listening with an open heart, really taking on board where the other is coming from, means you really do understand their point of view and can tell them that and give them that recognition and appreciation.

The little things held inside, which are a build up of energy and interruptions to energy flow, are then released daily through the relationship dynamic, keeping a flow of love and the connection.

No Thanks, No Sorry, Between Us

When there is such a strong flow of acceptance and love of one for the other, new deeper experiences of love await—beyond your imagining. No Thanks, No Sorry, was something I couldn't conceive of, but we discovered this dynamic further along our path.

My husband says to me, "No thanks, no sorry, between us, delete these words from our dictionary."

If anyone has to apologise in our relationship it's me. What I mean is, I'm the one most likely to get stressed and will speak and act from emotion, and I'm more likely to say something I regret later. My husband just listens and absorbs it all. Then he says, "What else?" He lets me rant on a bit more, really listening without interruption until there is nothing else. Then he answers me. He doesn't even react if I say something that might hurt him along the way. What this means is, the release of my energy is completely unobstructed, he allows me to express how I feel, absorbs it all, and lets it go. We don't end up in a shouting match or a battle to be heard, with each interrupting the other. One speaks the other listens. Having been allowed to do that, with everything clear in me from the inside, I have the space to reflect on the interaction and can see what I said and how I may have hurt him by my words. I go back to say, "I'm sorry for what I said; I think that may have hurt you." He says, "No sorry; I accept everything from you." What he means is, what I said didn't hurt him; he accepted and released it. If there was no injury done, i.e. no energy got stuck so there is no need for an apology. Such is his acceptance, such is his flow. He says "I accept everything from you until the end of my life" and I feel and know that I am in the presence of great love.

Also, when he does something for me or says something appreciative to me and I say "thank you," he now says, "no thanks needed." For most of us, we like to have thanks and appreciation and if we don't get it, we sometimes feel resentful. This comes from our 'need' for appreciation in return for what we gave. For him, it's completely freely given, there is no need. He doesn't just say it. This is how it is for him. This is how his energy system is working.

This kind of love and acceptance was beyond the possibility of my imagining. But this has grown through living out these principles of acceptance and nourishment of each other. I have done it consciously, my husband has just responded and transformed accordingly, my energy dynamics creating changes and transformation in him and now I am the beneficiary of this great and wonderful heart of his. He knew nothing of energy flow and energy nutrition but he came

| Diagram 7 | Paying attention, listening with an open heart is a release path for the energy of another. |

into a relationship with someone who did, and now through unconscious learning he is a master himself.

Paying attention, Listening and Acceptance together with Recognition and Appreciation are the keys to deepening the flow and connection between you. Seek to create opportunities to spend some time together connecting in this way to allow it to happen.

Diagram 8   Soothing balm of recognition and appreciation helps to release and soothe person's energy system.

It Only Takes One Person to Change

The problem in relationships is that if both people are stressed, then neither has the capacity to handle the other's situation. Each energy system is blocked and neither can see past their own emotional experience to consider the other's position. Interruptions while the other is trying to speak and shouting matches ensue, leading to switching off, avoidance and no-go subjects, or other escalatory behaviour in order to be heard.

One person has to make a change. That's all it takes to then change the energy dynamics of the relationship.

Who has to change? The one reading this book is the one with the knowledge, or the one who has the desire for something to change, the 'bigger' person—bigger meaning the one with greater capacity in their energy system, or who has the desire to create that. So if both parties are stressed, then one should take some time out to release that pressure of the build up of energy within themselves in order to be free and more relaxed and to increase their capacity to pay attention to their partner. That's where self-help techniques come in. It's also where an ET Buddy is invaluable, or an ET Practitioner as a back up if you have been carrying a lot of pressure for a long time. It's totally ok to ask for help. For those who are asked to help, it's usually an honour to be asked. Using the techniques in Exercise 12: Deepending Your Love, is a good way to change the energy of a relationship.

"For a flower to blossom, offering its beauty and perfume
year after year for you to enjoy, it needs more than water and minerals,
it needs the attention of the sun.

The food and drink on their table is not enough.

Your heart energy is the sunshine of your relationship"

Deepening Your Love

Think of ways that you can put into practice the following:

Paying Attention, Listening

Really look at your partner, really notice them, who they are, what they do, how they are feeling.

Really listen when they are talking to you. Try not to interrupt when they need to talk, let them finish.

Acceptance

Invite in the energy of your partner, when they are in a good mood, soften and flow and let go, feel the joy of who they are.

Invite in the energy of your partner, when they are not feeling so good, soften and flow where you feel that in your body. Really listen, absorb, and take in what's going on for or them and release it.

Recognition

Now you understand how they are feeling or you can see them for who they really are because you've read their energy with your whole being. You felt that in your heart.

Appreciation

Tell them what you see, tell them what you appreciate.

Think of other what ways you can express your appreciation, in words by speaking from the heart, through actions showing kindness and thoughtfulness, and through touch.

Just as you put out food on the table every day, make it a habit to recognise and appreciate something in your partner regularly. You are building a strong heart energy and a strong flow in your partner, of which you will also be the beneficiary as that love comes back to you.

Consideration

Consideration is being open and able to take in the energy and situation of another person, absorb that, understand that, and then respond and act accordingly with that knowledge. But if you are stressed and blocked yourself, you cannot see past your own issues and you cannot therefore allow another person's situation in to be understood. So soften and release your stress, that you may be able to be considerate to your partner.

Exercise 15: Heart Healing and Nutrition (page 116) in Chapter 30: Falling in Love With Yourself, and Exercise 19: Healing Our Relationship With Our Physical Body (page 128) in Chapter 32: Loving Your Perfect Body, would be a beautiful exercises to do with your partner. This brings physical touch, love and appreciation together as a powerful energy nutrition.

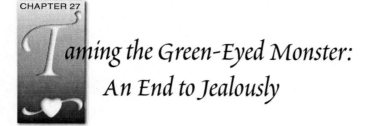

CHAPTER 27

Taming the Green-Eyed Monster: An End to Jealously

*J*ealousy can be a problem for both partners in a relationship. For the one who feels jealous, that's not a nice experience. For the other partner, the jealousy feel like possessiveness, restricting your freedom.

Verbal reassurance from one to the jealous partner is not enough because there are real energetic injuries behind those strong emotions; there area reasons for that insecurity that need to be repaired and released.

Steve and Becky

Steve and Becky had been together many years and they had a son who was six years old. Their relationship had been strong until Becky had gone on a trip with a male work colleague for a meeting away from home. This work colleague was a successful confident guy, who had a nice car, nice bike and a nice lifestyle. When Steve asked Becky about him, she wasn't very open about details of her colleague's life. She said she hadn't really asked him much during the journey. But Steve felt she was being evasive. Suddenly Steve started to feel anxious and concerned about how Becky was dressing, which was a lot nicer than her usual style going to work. He commented about this. He started to ask her questions about her male work colleagues. Becky was not saying much and was starting to feel a bit restricted by her partner's constant questions about who she was with and where she was going, as he was seeking greater reassurance. Rather than make them closer, his over-anxious concerns were making her want her space more. But Steve just couldn't help it.

Steve came to see me. We started to explore the feelings in his body when he thought of her clothes, the men at work, this guy, Luke, she'd gone to that meeting with. We cleared the energy, which was tightness in the chest and abdomen. What came up for him was that his ex-wife did have an affair and the name of that guy was Luke, the same name as Becky's colleague, and that since that overnight meeting away, all his old insecurities and hurt from this last relationship had been triggered. Although on the one hand, he had no reason to distrust Becky, still certain behaviours were triggering the old anxiety and pain and fear of rejection and abandonment. So I used the techniques in Exercise 13: Jealousy and Insecurity (page 100), to help Steve.

We returned to the events around his ex-wife leaving, and released all this fear and pain, and worked on him loving himself more. He left feeling great. The next visit, he said he felt more comfortable now with Becky and her buying a nice black dress for the work's party didn't bother him as he thought it might. He just felt sad and guilty that he'd allowed his past to cause a problem in his current relationship. So we released this sadness from his chest and the guilt from his head and stomach.

I then asked, "How much do you trust Becky now?"

There was a tiny mistrust feeling still in his heart. We cleared this until he said, "I feel fine now. She needs some space to express herself and I can accept that. I don't feel anxious any more; I feel more secure."

Another common dynamic with a client experiencing jealousy was the discomfort at seeing his partner giving her attention to another man, however innocent, and not giving that attention to him. That discomfort in the stomach also had to be softened and released, which then allowed him to be more relaxed and accepting about that.

Jealousy and Insecurity

Letting Go of Jealousy and Insecurity

Think about the situations or behaviours involving your partner that make you feel jealous and insecure. For each one, note where you feel that in your body, breathe into it, let it soften, flow, and release.

Remember when you experienced a sense of betrayal or infidelity. Take each incident in turn, locate the feeling in your body, let it soften, flow, and release. When you have released painful memories, return to the present and think again about those behaviours your partner exhibits and notice how you feel about them now. If there is anything remaining to clear, breathe into it and think of it softening and flowing until it's released.

Once you have cleared this issue for yourself, realise the effect it has had on your partner. Talk about it open heart to open heart. Take turns speaking and listening until you have cleared any remaining energy between you.

Handling Jealousy and Insecurity

If you are with a partner who is jealous and possessive, the way you handle it can help them to release that insecurity and to feel more secure. Your ability to accept and understand the behaviour and discuss it openly with your partner will help, whereas if your feelings of restriction remain, then your need for more space and freedom will only perpetuate the situation for your partner.

Think of a situation where your partner's jealousy is a problem for you. Note how you feel. Where do you feel that in your body? Soften and flow.

Think of another situation where your partner's jealousy is problem for you. Where do you feel that? Soften and flow.

Repeat until you can handle this behaviour from your partner.

Healing Each Other

Now that you feel less stressed and more relaxed, you can help your partner to release this problem. Sit down and talk to you partner and ask them to express how they feel. Ask them what behaviours in you are a problem for them? Make a list.

For each item ask, "Where do you feel that anxiety in your body?" Guide them to soften and release this energy.

If memories of past infidelities come up, take them one by one. For each one, recall what happened, ask where do they feel this in their body?

Help them to soften and release this old injury until no parts of the memory have any pain associated with it.

Being able to work together to help each other heal is a very nurturing and can help to deepen the love and trust between you. The simplicity of EmoTrance means that anyone can learn how to help another by simply identifying where the "problem" is located, and guiding their partner to soften and release this energy to restore The Even Flow.

CHAPTER 28

*W*hen Good Times Go Bad

I originally called this chapter Letting Go of The Good Times. Now why ever do we have to "let go" of the good times?

What we are talking about is the great highlight moments of our life, so great that we take that energy in and hold onto it, treasuring it. Life goes on and its never quite as good as that again. We seek it, we try to recreate it, we are let down, our expectations not met. Then this old memory becomes painful to recall, as it shows us not only what we once had, but the pain we experience because we never had it again.

Holding on to the good times is holding a particular energy, however good it feels in your heart, and this causes a blockage and disruption to healthy energy flow. This has a number of consequences.

1. We stop the flow of more of this kind of energy and great experience being attracted to us.

2. Our attempts to re-create and re-live these highlights can lead to high expectations in future relationships, which can cause further problems. In extreme cases our whole life can be driven by the aim to recreate this highlight moment in our lives. Silvia Hartmann refers to this phenomenon as a "Guiding Star."

3. The energy nourishment you were intended to receive in the original wonderful event is locked in the energy digestive system and is not delivered to the rest of the energy body. These highlight experiences have the power to transform us on a deep level, but this transformation and evolution is blocked by our holding on.

Let's have a look at these consequences in more detail with a few illustrations. Like everyone, I send and receive text messages a lot. And I keep the nice ones that I receive, especially the love texts. Well, my mobile phone has a certain capacity in the inbox, and when it gets full, any new messages can't come in. The same in our energy system, we have to keep the flow going so we can continue to attract more of the same.

My Phone Memory Was Full of Old Love Texts

I remember after a past relationship I still had some of those old love messages in my phone, months after it had ended. I used to look at them now and again, and I would reconnect with those good feelings, feeling nostalgic for my past romance. I kept them because it was the first time I'd received love messages like that. After my first EmoTrance training where I learned the principles of energy flow, I realised what I was doing, so that night at the hotel with my friend Kath, I decided to delete them all. But I tell you it was not easy. I remember standing there with my finger on the button ready to delete the first one and really not wanting to. As I pressed delete, it actually felt like something was being ripped from my stomach. I breathed, softened and flowed to release that energy I was holding. Kath was encouraging me to breathe, focus, soften and flow. Then the next one was difficult too; breathe, soften and flow, then by the fourth one they got easier. But the interesting thing was that with each release of that energy that I was holding in my heart and stomach, I gained more and more energy myself. It was dramatic and incredible. I was amazed! I had this sense of such freedom, release, energy and such happiness through my whole body; I was on a high literally for weeks. Wow, it really was a surprise how much I gained from letting go!

He Couldn't Live Up to My Expectations

I was running a Love Clinic workshop in Europe and when I talked about letting go of the past, even the good times, one participant said she never really got over her previous relationship, which had some really good times. Even though she was happy enough with her present husband, she would get angry as he continually failed to live up to her expectations of how it could be, based on how it was in the past. I directed her in the partner exercises to focus on the good times in her past relationship, to locate the energy in her body, to soften and release it with the help of a partner in the group. The next day she shared with the group what had changed between her and her husband since that release. She no longer had these high expectations, which also meant she could accept and appreciate her husband for who he actually was, as opposed to resenting who he wasn't. This deepened their connection and they were both so much happier for it.

The Diamond Transformation

Here is an extraordinary case story contributed by Silvia Hartmann, creator of EmoTrance. The story is about a moment of intense love, experienced 30 years ago; a moment that should have been an instant transformation of the person who experienced it, but was not because they took the energy and "enfolded it within their heart." They kept it there as a keepsake of the best moment in their lives. And there it remained and stopped any further flow or experience of something similar or even better happening to this person. It ruined this person's life entirely in the process by keeping them stuck in the past. What happened when they understood that they must complete the process that was started all those years ago?

Completing the Diamond Transformation

Silvia says:

> I know we probably know this about ET by now, but even I was really blown away by doing this spontaneous treatment with someone on a— well, I guess you can call it a 'super issue.'
>
> The life defining deal, the real big thing, which happened over 30 years ago and spawned innumerable symptoms, related occurrences, formed life patterns, belief structures and values hierarchies, had the deepest possible tie-ins with people and objects—it was a huge big deal in all.
>
> Now, this 'super issue' had, at the core of it, a massive Guiding Star. All the rest of the life problem grew around this, as is so often the case with such experiences. Basically the person in question had been holding on for dear life to this memory/energy and had built their lives more or less like a shrine around this Guiding Star memory.
>
> The idea turned up one day that they were weary of their role as the priest to that temple they'd build to the single experience. But there was no way they could let it go. Even though it was as clear as anything that they would be wasting the rest of their lives, just as successfully in that function and set-up as they had done so far with what had been going on for the previous 30 years, unless they would allow this system to become liquid and 'let it go' at last.
>
> Talk about resistance to the very idea! Wow. That was really something. The emotional responses, pleading and absolute refusal that followed—just everything in full out reversal at the mere suggestion that letting go of this would be a good thing, was surprising.
>
> So I actively took this whole deal and switched it into the energy world view. Here, what we had was not emotions and love and contortions and entanglements and constructs and feedback loops and and and and and; but instead was this total clarity and simplicity of an energy that they had enfolded and held in their heart.
>
> Literally, in their heart.
>
> An energy that was so intense and so dense that it was hard as a diamond, and if anyone would try to remove this, the person would fear that

their 'heart was being torn from their chest,' and rightfully so, as the diamond had grown into the very structure of their energetic heart.

And in this view of clarity and logic, it was incontrovertible that this diamond represented a structural problem of great proportions; that it physically and practically *entirely blocked the flow of any kind of energy* through the heart; that the systems below and around were parched and atrophied for the lack of flowing, living energy; and even that this energy had *never done what it should have done* to the entirety of the system *because it did not complete its pathways* and did not ever complete the entirely positive and beneficial transformation to the energy body its movement through the system would have initiated.

From this viewpoint of clarity and logic, there was simply no doubt as to what had happened.

It wasn't a tragedy.

It wasn't a blessing.

It wasn't Karma and it wasn't God's will.

It wasn't all those contorted meanings or anything at all, it was simply there, cause and effect, with the pathways to what needed to be done laid out in crystal clarity for everyone to see, to understand, to appreciate.

There was no doubt at all as to what needed to be done, and no resistance at all to having it happen—it was so perfectly and so clearly the right thing to do, the *only* thing to do that the person spontaneously said with complete conviction, "The transformation has to be completed, the diamond energy must be allowed to move."

As the person began immediately and without *any hesitation* to soften the very outside layers and ingrown connections to have them rise like mist and begin their journey through the dust dry pathways and channels that had not been used for 30 years, I was watching them with a sense of amazement and awe.

This was the same person who had thought that they could not ever let go of this; that it was the only thing in this life for them and they could never hope for anything better.

This was the same person who had virtually fought to the brink of death to protect the diamond in their heart from any intervention by any healer, psychologist, therapist, well meaning friend and from themselves, too.

This was the same person who now, after just *one look* at the clarity and logic of the energetic realities in their energy body was feeling the 30 year old diamond energy beginning to rush through the channels in their body, beginning to breathe faster and glow, trembling as the transformation, which had begun all that time ago, finally was allowed to be completed right in front of my eyes.

They were absolutely at a loss for words afterwards and so was I.

We were just sitting there, looking at each other and this strange sense of epiphany? rebirth? righting a wrong? holiness? was right there with us in the room and nothing needed to be said—what could you say to that?

I came away from that with a whole new-found respect for the basic principles of ET and a whole new respect for how that simple switch into the viewpoint of energy and flow had simply side-stepped all the energetic injuries, all the emotional pain entanglements, all the beliefs and decisions, all the thought constructs designed to protect the status quo and to make some sense of it.

And in this place of clarity and logic, how there was a compassion to be found that totally touched both the person and myself so intensely. This was not a cold and barren place, bereft of feelings—on the contrary, it was a holy space; a space of awe that takes your breath away.

Now that's what I call energy healing.

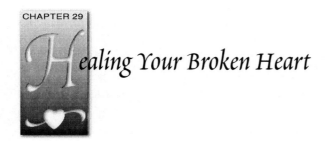

CHAPTER 29

Healing Your Broken Heart

*T*he loss of a loved one is a huge energetic event to process. We go through stages of grieving from shock and denial, to pain and loss and eventually on to acceptance peace grace and love.

But for some, they cannot grieve, they never had the chance, due to responsibilities on them at the time, or the fear of processing and dealing with such a huge energy, so they held it back.

Others accept, feel the pain, but cannot let go, as the pain is a connection to their lost beloved and a fear of losing that connection if they don't have the pain.

For those who have the courage to accept and to process all aspects of this event as it happens and also face and process the consequences of their life going on without their loved one; for those who do allow themselves to feel and to allow the energy to flow and to release, they can experience deep love for the departed and a joy and gratitude for their life.

Understanding how to transform emotional energy is a powerful tool and support to help us through such big life events. Knowing that our painful emotions are only energy that we can soften and release helps us cope better and process events more easily. There is not only the pain of loss but there is the pain associated with the beautiful memories also, which we can gently release allowing us to experience the beauty and gratitude without the pain.

Also understanding that a major source of a person's energy nutrients, their source of love and care is no longer there. Being able to accept the love and support of others is important at this time, and to develop other ways to nourish ourselves, if we had become dependent on our partner. Taking in the nourishment of nature, friends, family and learning to love ourselves more and to receive spiritual nourishment through our relationship with Source, in whatever form that takes is important for our continued health and well-being. Again, understanding how to really absorb that and allow all those energies to feed and sustain us will help us so much through this time.

Social convention and our human experience so far tell us 'it should take a certain length of time to grieve.' Yes, but we can help to speed this process to reach our final healing and deep transformation from this experience because, however big it is, its still an energetic event, or series of energetic events to process, and as such all the principles of energy flow and energy nutrition apply.

Lessening and releasing the pain of loss doesn't mean we forget. It means that the pain of remembrance is transformed to acceptance, peace, gratitude and love.

Shock and Denial at News of Bereavement

I was giving EmoTrance training and during the event one of the group, Alice, received news that her mother had died. She wasn't as close to her mother as her sister was, and her mother lived in France, while Alice was in England. She was stunned by this news. Thank God she is at an EmoTrance training I thought. I offered to help her to process this privately after the workshop finished.

Alice was in shock and she said it didn't feel real. She had a shield protecting her from the full impact of this event. That's why she couldn't feel it.

We identified where the shield was.

"All of this news and all that it means, where does it exist? Scan around you, and point to it," I requested.

She pointed. "Far away over there. Now I'm feeling scared about looking at it. It's so big I don't know if I can handle it," she said. All this anxiety was now in her chest and throat. We softened and flowed and released it. So now she was ready to handle the news and what it meant.

Using the approach for shields, we made a tiny hole in the shield to allow her to experience a tiny bit of that energy, and to clear the energy disturbances in her system that it triggered, until it could flow out. Bit by bit we increased the flow of energy softening and flowing along the way.

Lots of thoughts came up for Alice in the process. We eventually arrived at a place where she could accept and say comfortably, "My mother has died," and to feel peaceful and loving about that.

Then there were more issues—that her mum never hugged her, and they weren't close. She had regrets about this, and the problems her mother had, and how Alice had handled it then. We located and released all the energy about these emotionally charged issues until Alice was able to think of her mum with love and great compassion.

The next day Alice was calm, present, open and still in a space of loving acceptance. I suggested that as time went on there would be more thoughts and memories that came up about her mum, which would trigger her emotions, and she should deal with them in the same way: to breathe into it, soften and to release the energy.

I felt that Alice had handled the first big wave of this enormous news beautifully. She was awesome in her compassion and love and strength and shining beauty that she got from it all. It was humbling to witness and a privilege to facilitate and be present at. Alice went home and was just fine, handling the ongoing family issues that needed to be faced with total grace and love.

When My Brother-in-Law Died

Using the techniques in Exercise 14: Letting Go and Healing, helped me to deal with a sudden and tragic incident which left my brother in law so brain damaged with no chance of any conscious normal life. The painful decision was made with the support of the hospital to turn off his life support. It was a tragedy; he was in his late thirties, had two kids, and he was going. I stood around the hospital bed with my sister, brother and my brother-in-law's family. It was a highly emotionally charged time, watching him as he struggled with his last breaths until his body gave up and he departed. Everyone was in tears. I too felt the waves of emotion swelling. I breathed, softened and flowed. Then another wave: I breathed, softened and flowed. And another wave: breathe, soften and flow. I felt an enormous love for him, and great compassion for the family around us. Somehow I managed to transform this intense emotional moment to a state of pure grace. I will never forget the sacredness of that moment, and every time I recall it still I feel that profound love and grace. There was more to handle in terms of how his children received the news. That was more painful to witness. I breathed into the pain, softened and flowed. The next day as everyone was still raw and tearful I was more than surprised to find myself quite calm, relaxed and free. For me, it was as if it was weeks later, as if I had processed it already. In fact, that was exactly what had happened. At the enormity of the event, as it happened, while the impact of the wave was hitting us all, I dealt with that wave fully as it was happening. For my family, the emotions were still intense, and would be for some time yet. The wave of energy was still locked in their energy bodies, as they did not have the capacity or ability to handle it all at the time. The energy remained to be triggered by many thoughts through the day, but for me the wave had passed.

There were many times that were difficult for the children. At seven and three it was a lot to handle. My sister was great at allowing them to talk about their dad whenever they wanted and allowing them to feel and express their emotions, giving them lots of hugs and reassurance, and with time things got easier. There were other ways that I helped. I tuned in to my nephew's great sadness about losing his dd. Where do I feel his deep sadness and loss in my body? I asked myself. There it was in my chest, I softened and flowed and let it go. It helped. I saw how he became easier and more able to cope. My niece went through a clingy phase, not wanting her mum to go out, crying as she went out of the door, and at three, having insecurities now about losing her mum too. I tuned in. Where do I feel her great fear of losing her

Letting Go and Healing

As the energies you have to deal with are often quite enormous during bereavement, I strongly recommend seeking help from an experienced practitioner. However, alongside this, you can also help yourself on a daily basis with the following exercises.

Please remember that any amount of energy that you manage to release will help lessen the load. So don't worry if you don't release it all at once. As you increasingly restore the flow within your sense of peace and love will increase.

Letting Go

When Painful Thoughts Come

Breathe into the pain, soften and flow

When you look at Pictures and there's pain

Breathe into the pain, soften and flow

When you recall certain memories

Breathe into the pain, soften and flow

When you think of difficult events ahead that you have to face

Breathe into the pain, soften and flow

When you think of the good times

Breathe into the pain, soften and flow

As you transform the pain softening into The Even Flow, your complete the transformation within you that was intended by that energy, by that experience. You receive the deeper nourishment as was intended. Letting go profoundly enriches your spirit.

Nourishment and Renewal

Seek to receive nourishment from all the sources around you:

Sunshine

Go out in the sunshine. Feel the sun on your skin, feel the strength and power of the sun's energy, invite it into your body, soften and flow until you feel that strengthening within.

Nature

Go into a garden or a park, look at the plants and trees, invite their energies in, soften and flow, feel the nourishment within

People Around You

Friends and family can be a great support and help, but you need to let them in. Opening up to receive kindness and love from others can be painful while there are still major energetic injuries within to be repaired. Know that you can feel the pain, breathe into it, soften and flow.

Exercise continued on next page

Remember "If you can bear to feel it, you can heal it'

Yourself

The Heart Healing Prayer can be a great grounding meditation to bring you back to your centre and help you to start to nourish yourself

The Heart Healing Prayer

I place my healing hands

On my heart of energy,

To heal what once was broken,

To make right what once went wrong,

To soften and to flow,

To restore the Even Flow,

So that my heart of energy,

Can once again,

Shine like the Sun.

When you are ready you can give yourself deeper nourishment with Exercise 15: Heart Healing and Nutrition, on page 116.

Your Source

If you have a relationship with Source/God/Allah/Spirit/The Creator/Jesus then ask to receive the nourishment and healing that you need from that Source. When you pray, you invoke those Divine energies which are deeply healing so that you can receive them and let them flow in and through. Be aware of feelings in your body, soften and flow to deepen your experience.

mum in my body? I asked myself. In my heart. I softened and flowed. Her behaviour became less anxious. She became more secure and able to let her Mum go out without a fuss. Whilst trying to lighten their emotional load, I also got something myself: greater compassion and greater capacity to love.

Two years on, with a lot of family support and love, they are once again two happy radiant children, with their spirits shining bright again—a total joy to behold.

We Can Be a Channel of Release for Another

Notice how I used my own energy system as a channel for the release of the emotional energy of my niece and nephew on those occasions. This dynamic of relationships was explained earlier, how complete acceptance of the other's emotional state and energy allows some release through the channel of the person accepting. By asking, "Where do I feel this person's sadness in my body?" what we are doing is inviting the energy of their state into our own system, healing anything within us that stops it flowing, then letting it flow in through and release out through us, thereby allowing some release of pressure in the other person.

The fact that this works also shows the importance of us being able to handle whatever is going on for another person. While we can't handle it and we feel the emotional pain of another person, or we block it out completely, avoiding it, this blockage within us is blocking one of their channels of release. They will carry that distress for longer. Our openness and acceptance helps another to release their energy more easily; i.e., just by being the presence of love and offering that open hearted acceptance to others is helping them to heal.

These stories show us ways that we can help to ease ourselves or another person through this challenging time. If you have experienced bereavement, do seek some help from an EmoTrance Practitioner who can assist and support you to gently and respectfully release some of the pressure you are feeling. Meanwhile some of the suggestions in the exercises below may help you on a daily basis.

CHAPTER 30

Falling in Love With Yourself

We all need a constant stream of Energy Nutrients in, through and out of the system. The most important or sought after energy nutrients are Attention, Recognition, Appreciation and Love. This is essential for good health and well-being, just as important as a wide variety of foods in our physical diet.

Healing and Feeding the Heart Energy Centre

Now, it's all very well if we have got someone to give us recognition and appreciation all the time. But most of us are not in that situation and the deficiency we are in causes us to seek those nutrients in our relationships with others.

If we have a partner who is generally loving and attentive, that's great, but maybe sometimes they are just too tired, depressed or a bit stressed and they haven't got that available for us at our time of need; they just can't give us the support and the security that we want. Then we are disappointed, hurt and resentful. If it goes on for a period of time, our hurt and resentment can build into, "Well I give up" and to seek that attention elsewhere or just to close down to the partner, to stop the feelings of hurt.

This 'need' for Energy Nutrients arising from our deficiency can put a strain on relationships. It's possible to live with them some of the time, but it can be felt as demanding and needy from the partner who is expected to provide in the moment when they can't, because they are busy dealing with their own stresses and as a result don't have the resources to give at that moment. Many people are in this pattern of looking for 'what they need' in their relationship, namely, Love.

How did we get to be so deficient?

Energy shields and barriers, energetic injuries in our energy system, from life experiences and events we are still holding stop the steady flow of energy nutrients in through and out. Instead of feeling good when someone appreciates us and shows us a kindness, some of us feel pain, as the energy flows in and hits an old injury in the system, triggering the old emotions. If we have shields, then we don't feel anything at all. EmoTrance gives us an easy way of softening and releasing those old injuries, and the chapter on Shields explains how we approach taking them down.

For whatever reason, we are as we are now, but now we can choose something different for ourselves from this moment and as a consequence of how we change and learn, we can choose something different for others and for the next generation.

The Heart Energy Centre is not some pink and fluffy thing. It's the power centre of our spiritual person. When it's well fed and strong, we are open, courageous, we radiate love and warmth.

Some time ago, Silvia Hartmann introduced the concept of Heart Healing— feeding and nourishing the heart. I took it to another level as a few minutes of heart healing wasn't nearly enough for me. I felt soothed, grounded and balanced, but I needed more. So I started with a poem that Silvia wrote along the lines of "What Every Person Needs."

ᘛ

What Every Person Needs

What every person needs as a human being is really,
Just one single person to be absolutely on our side,
To really love us, help us, protect us, inspire us,
Applaud us when we have succeeded in something,
No matter how insignificant it may seem to an outsider;
Someone who will encourage us to strive towards
The best we can possibly be,
Someone who will always cheer us on;
Someone who cannot ever be tempted away
By youth, beauty, money, bribes;
Someone who will always choose us,
Every day, each moment afresh;

Someone to stand by us when everything falls apart,
To Love us no matter what;
Someone who will never let us down, never give up on us,
Never leave us and who will always, always be
Fiercely and actively loving of us in every way, every day,
Until we take our last breath in
physicality.

Well, that person is here.
It is you.
And now, finally, we can start on the road to be that person we always knew
         we should have been…
With a little help from our Self, our endlessly loving totality.

ᘛ

I was reading this, thinking that "Yep, he hasn't arrived yet. Does such a perfect man exist?" But when I got to the end of the poem, there it was—that someone is YOU! That hit me—bam!—I was stunned for two weeks! It literally took me two weeks just to come round, reeling, from that. This person is me; I am the one who is supposed to love myself. How do I do that? I had read the books telling me to go for walks, take a lavender bath with candles etc, but this didn't work for me. I did not 'feel' that I loved myself anymore sitting in a bath with candles. How do I get the love, that feeling of love inside me? Something else needed to happen, but I didn't know how to do it.

When Silvia introduced this concept of how to heal the heart it was about feeding yourself, having a way to nourish yourself and to put that energy, those loving intentions, into your energy system to feed yourself. I finally got around to doing something about this.

One night I went to bed, put my hands on my heart to do this heart healing thing, to greet myself, to start to recognise and appreciate myself. The first time I did it, giving myself all those things that I was looking for in somebody else. I had this lovely warm feeling, but I noticed that it was around the top half of my body. It wasn't anywhere else. I knew that I should be EmoTrancing this to soften and flow it away, but it felt soooo good that I didn't want to release it. I thought I'll just hold onto this for now, for a few days—I'll EmoTrance it next time.

I went around for a few days feeling really great, feeling good about myself, really happy then I thought I would have another go, this time doing it properly, to see what would happen. So that evening, I put my hands on my heart again, I connected in with myself, and again I started to feel nourished. I was just saying, "Sandra; you are…" I went on and on, giving myself all the things I was looking for; all the things that I wanted someone to say to me I said to myself instead. All the things that I would like from a relationship I gave those intentions and energies to myself. With the energy, the nourishment that I got energetically in my heart and chest area, this time I used EmoTrance to soften and flow. The energy spread and went all through my system and I let it go. It released down through my feet and up and out through my head. Then I went back and fed myself all over again, all those things I was looking for and realised that in fact there was now an unlimited supply of this love. I could do this whenever and for however long and as often as I wanted. Wow!

Do you know what happened with that strong flow and that nourishment to my spirit? I fell in love—with myself! It was amazing, I was in love—and not a man in sight! And every time I went to bed I was in rapture going to meet myself, my beloved, my intimate Self; what joy. Every night, it was wonderful! Then, obviously, the love that I had for myself extended out to everywhere. I loved everyone and everything and there was plentiful supply. The rapture of Love—I knew what this felt like.

Of all the things that I have done and learned about transforming emotional energy with EmoTrance, some of the most important things for me have been dropping my shields and barriers and understanding energy principles that energy needs to flow, everyone needs energy nutrition. But Heart Healing and building my heart energy has been by far the biggest and most important learning and transformation. I say transformation, because from that day onwards I was permanently changed.

When you build the heart energy and are well nourished and loved yourself, does it matter now if your partner is feeling a bit down and can't give it to you today? No—because you are so nourished you have all that you 'need' and now you have all the patience and the acceptance so you are not seeking it from them. Instead, you are able to offer to them what they need at that time: attention, acceptance, understanding, and a little soothing balm of recognition and appreciation.

I did the Heart Healing Transformation before I met my life partner. I was already happy. I had all the love I needed anyway. I became all those things to myself that I was seeking. And then what happened? I attracted a person into my life who had the capacity to be all those things to me. Talk about icing on the cake! Wow, the power of the Law of Attraction. I became all the things I wanted. I had what I wanted, then all those things came into my life from my partner anyway, now my beloved husband. I'm still in awe when I think of that. How to use the Law of Attraction to find the perfect partner. That's worth a book in itself!

Beginning Your Heart Healing and Transformation Journey

What I would like to share with you now is the process that I did for me and that you can do for yourself. You can do it once or you can do it several times. Perhaps you might need to do it quite often for a while, until you are able to get such a flow going and such an open and strong heart energy that just needs a little top up now and again. See Exercise 15: Heart Healing and Nutrition (page 116).

I do this heart healing process with my clients also. I use the poem as a trigger. Sometimes we sit and read through it. For some clients just reading the poem triggers their hurts and desires and disappointments; what they are looking for in their partners that they are not getting in their relationships. We do a little bit of soften and flow to clear the main energetic injuries first and then we go through the Heart Healing process using the concepts of the poem to help them start to nourish themselves, which is a wonderful thing, creating much change in themselves and their relationships.

Recognising that all of those things that you need—that we all need—for healthy functioning, all of that attention, recognition and appreciation, the love that we need and can give to ourselves, here is a way that we can directly nourish our

Heart Healing and Nutrition

I'd like you to take a deep breath, place you hands on where you feel is the centre of you, where your energy heart is. Take a moment to greet yourself; meet with yourself in whatever way that feels right. I just usually say, "Hi, it's me, I'm here...at last." Just take a moment to appreciate yourself—you may want to do it silently, but if you are alone and can say the words out loud and use your name, the energy is much more powerful this way. As you say each line, directing the intentions into your heart, give yourself a chance to receive the full energy of those words. Absorb it.

Do this for yourself, or you may find it helpful for a partner to guide you with the words. If you need it, an EmoTrance Practitioner will be able to assist you.

So, hey, here I am...I am here for you...
I am the one here to support you...
I appreciate you...
And all your wonderful qualities...
I can see how good you are...
How strong you are...
How talented you are....
How kind you are...
How gentle you are...
How caring and considerate you are....
How generous you are...
How courageous you are...
How you always try so hard to do your best....I see that
I understand you....

If any of these words trigger your emotions, or you have a surge of energy running through your body, just notice where it is, and put your attention there. Let it soften and flow. Then just return back to the process.

Again, I appreciate you...
I see who you are...
I see what a wonderful, adorable, amazing person that you are...
I completely love you,
I adore you,
You're amazing,
You're perfect...just as you are...
You don't have to change, I love you just as you are
<say your name to yourself>...I love you...

I want you to put your attention to behind your hands, maybe you have already noticed there is a warm energy feeling building up there—put your attention there. I want you to think that this energy is softening and flowing... Just allow it soften and flow...Let it gently spread out...You might feel that warmth spreading out into your chest. Notice how far it's got, how far it wants to go, just feeling where it is, softening and flowing.

While that's flowing, come back again and just give yourself a little bit more appreciation.

I want you to now, silently, take a few moments just to say to yourself anything that you have been wanting to hear. Any words, any recognition, any appreciation, any support. I want you to give that to yourself now. Take your time.

Pay attention to what's going on in your body. What does that energy feel like now in your body? Just think of it softening and flowing; see now where else it wants to go. Maybe it wants to go up, but it can't. Is there anything stopping it? Let that area soften. Maybe it's going down but it has hit something, some other kind of obstacle. Just let it soften, let that energy flow. See if you can follow it, see if it spreads through your body, and beyond, until it is all releasing, so that you have a flow into your heart, through and out of all your energy system.

When you have that flow going, you can go back and give yourself even more. Tell yourself just how wonderful you are; just how amazing; just how completely loveable, amazing and wonderful you are. How strong; how courageous; how wise; how gentle...how completely shining and bright you are.

Again, direct that intention in to your heart centre, let it soften and flow through your energy system. Just recognise that there is an infinite, unlimited supply of all of this energy nutrition available to you whenever you need it. You just need to meet yourself and connect with yourself. Direct it inwards.

Gently, in your own time, take another moment or so if you feel that you need a little bit more, let it all soften and flow, releasing out of your whole system. When you're ready, in your own time, gently open your eyes, relax your hands and come back to the room.

Take a nice deep breath; just see how good that feels.

whole being. From that nourished state of flow and a strong heart, our need from others and our expectations of others are perhaps not as great now as they used to be. Perhaps now we can share a little bit more of that, we have got a little bit more to share, and a bit more attention, recognition and appreciation that we can give to others.

From our own state of flow we can accept people more easily, actually see and understand where people are coming from and give them what they need. We can be more considerate and demonstrate more care. When we are blocked we can't do that; when we are stressed we are literally stupid as we don't have access to all our resources, so we react from our emotional state. When we are in flow we can see, understand, and have a much wiser more considered and compassionate response to people. These actions are received by others more easily than our stressed emotional responses. This transforms our relationships to better communication, more heart connection, more spiritual nourishment and more love.

Building strong heart energy is not only about loving yourself and being able to love others more, it's also about courage. When the heart is strong and powerful, you are not afraid of life. You speak and live from the heart with openness, honesty and ease. People see that and that radiant energy is attractive. You no longer need your shields. The powerful heart energy and the flow in your energy system is its own defence. Whatever comes our way we can handle well, with compassion warmth and love. We learn and become enriched; we have understanding and develop wisdom; we have courage now where once there was fear.

Men often fear opening their hearts because society has taught them it's weak to feel their emotions. She they are more often shielded and closed. But beyond the difficult emotions, when we can handle that well, there is flow and the chance to build a strong heart power.

As we continue through life with this openness we can take so much more of life in, and experience it fully. This, in turn, enriches us more and makes us stronger still. We increase our capacity for life. The more of life's energies we can ingest, digest and release, the more enriched we become as a human; the heart grows yet stronger. This is the Lion Heart energy of great and wise leaders and great teachers—and of great love—and you can start now to build and nurture this for yourself.

Common Questions on Heart Healing

But won't I become arrogant taking all those affirmations in?

Only if you hold on to the energy. Letting that energy in and through then releasing it, gives you the nourishment you need. Holding onto it causes a blockage to the flow and deficiency in some parts of your energy system. This is what creates arrogance.

What about God and Jesus and receiving His love?

Yes, this is a nice way of re-framing the exercise. You could do the same exercise saying "God or Jesus is accepting me and loving me just as I am." Try it both ways and see what you learn from that.

I did the Heart Healing exercise and it was too emotional

When strong emotions are triggered, try to focus on where those emotions are coming from in the body. Soften and flow the energy, breathe through it. The energy will release and you can continue. If there are too many emotions being triggered, then you may wish to take some of the incoming energies of appreciation one by one, to be able to handle them. When you have developed more flow, you can return to the fully blown heart nutrition exercise.

I did the Heart Healing exercise and I felt nothing

This means the energy was not being accepted. Maybe you have some shields to accepting this kind of energy. Explore the space outside your body, and see if you can sense that the energy arrives so far and then stops. Using the approach taught in the shields exercise, allow a tiny amount in first, learn to handle that, then increasingly you can allow more and more energy in.

Who is the I? Who is doing the Loving to Who? Why the Duality?

This is a good question. We will explore this more when we look at Discovering the Real You. Briefly though, for most of us there is a difference between the You according to how you were designed as a spiritual person, and the You that you are living and experiencing right now. The energies of life events have been overlaid on the spirit body, held in the energy system, causing the lack and needs that you are experiencing right now, and which you are addressing through this exercise, and which you are healing through other exercises in this book. The Real You, is the You underneath all that blocked energy, the template you were given when you were conceived, which grows an develops as you mature, which functions in the Even Flow by design, and which is simultaneously part of, connected to, and a channel for Universal Energy, call that what you may. When we say "I love you" to ourselves, the 'I' is our true spiritual template, designed and therefore aligned and connected with Source or the Creative Order, and is the source or channel for the Love. The You is the what we call the 'autogenic spirit body,' the result of how we handled life so far, our belief systems, and how we are living as a result of that, the cloak over our naked spirit. Our intention is therefore to heal and release the autogenic body, to restore the Even Flow, and then 'I' and 'You' become the same. You then have no 'needs'—you are living love and joy.

$\mathcal{M}$eeting The Real You

$\mathcal{W}$e have seen how the energy causing negative emotions can be transformed into positive emotional states. We are designed with this ability and potential. We are designed to handle the energies of life, to transform them in this way, from fear to fun, from pain to joy, from sadness to laughter, from anger to love.

What stops us from doing this? What makes us live in the reactive emotional state? Well, firstly, some of us didn't know we could do anything about that until now. Secondly, our energy channels got blocked up, because we didn't know what to do with all those life events as they happened to us. All that blocked energy is now causing our emotional behaviour and creating our beliefs about the world, and therefore our judgement filters, barriers and limitations have also been established. That's what we are living out today.

But we were designed to be and to live better than that. Our innate structure of our energy system, of our spirit person, by design, allows us to flow these energies of life through us. This creative template allows us to gain something from them, to let the excesses go, with all those positive emotional states we have discussed, happiness, joy, clarity of vision, compassion, understanding, love, delight, rapture. We are designed to learn and grow on a spiritual level, i.e., engaging our totality as opposed to trying to work it all out in our poor overloaded conscious mind, which is only one part of the system. We are designed to be able to draw wisdom from what we learn through these deeper experiences.

Therefore, our potential is a life in flow. Finding role models in our society is not easy—someone to look up to, to aspire to be like, or to become. Who is your role model?

What about The Real You as your role model? Not the you that's living out all the blocked energy and emotional stress and painful past and judgement filters. The Real You; the You that was originally designed for you to be and to become. As we can have a perfectly healthy physical body, when everything is flowing well so we can process nutrition, digest, assimilate, metabolise, regenerate, release and eliminate, in the same way we can have a perfectly healthy spiritual body. Let's contemplate the perfectly healthy functioning of our Spirit person, our energy system, when all systems are flowing as they should: perfect Even Flow.

Exercise 16: Meeting the Real You (page 122) and Exercise 17: Seeing Another For Who They Truly Are (page 123), invite you to Meet the Real You, then to meet and see another human being for who they really are; their real potential inside. The Real You, which Silvia Hartmann calls "The Creative Template," is your role model, the person you should be aspiring to become. This is your potential. This is how you were designed to live and to be. And now, once you have had a glimpse of that, you can begin to move towards that, restoring the flow as you come closer and closer to the real you, your potential, your true spirit and all the possibilities that this brings.

Once you have connected with your true potential, remembering this experience, and all its flow states, you can see now what has to happen to move you closer to that: what repairs; what healing. You can also reconnect with that state and the resources you have available to you in that state at any time, when faced with a challenge. Simply ask, what would The Real You do in this situation?

Becoming aware of this concept in ourselves, and also starting to reach for that true spirit in another person, to feel what their energy is like, is also a totally joyful and amazing experience.

Meeting The Real You

Place your hands on your body on the place you feel is You, the Heart of You.

Make a wish that you now come to meet The Real You, your Creative Template, your birthright, your true potential. Contemplate for a moment that at the moment of your conception, there came into being a design for you, not just what you would grow to become physically, but also a template for your spirit, how you would function as a spiritual being.

Contemplate this spiritual you with an energy mind, an energy heart, a soul, energy centres, systems and channels for processing the energies of life, deriving nourishment from them, and releasing what is no longer required.

Contemplate how this spiritual you will feel when the whole system is in The Even Flow. When the heart is open, can accept, understand, be enriched and rejoice in life, and then let it go.

How would you feel in this life? How would you feel about yourself? How would your relationships work with that openness, acceptance, understanding, compassion, joy, happiness, the ability to handle all kinds of energies, with that kind of love?

What would you look like if you we living with this Even Flow? Would you wear the same kind of clothes? Women, would you wear make up and dye your hair? What energies are behind the need or desire for make up and cover up? With total self acceptance and love would you even bother? Would you be the same size or shape? What work would you be doing if you had no fear and total belief in yourself? How would you be spending your time in what work, what recreation? What would you be like? How would you feel in your life?

Take a moment to connect with this state of flow. It might be emotional for some. If it is, notice where you feel that energy, soften flow, breathe into it and let it go. Learn about this state, The Real You, Your Potential. Notice what resources are available to you when living as The Real You, how you act in life. Think of a challenge you are facing today. While connected with The Real You, notice how The Real You would handle that and what different resources The Real You has available to deal with that situation.

Make it your sincere desire and intention to move closer and closer to this You, the You that you know really is you, that is other than the you are living day to day right now. This You is your role model. And your journey of evolution is to be closer and closer to this until there is only The Real You.

Take a deep breath, relax your hands. Know that you can now reconnect with The Real You anytime you need to draw upon those resources when you need them. Know that when you observe yourself behaving in any way different from The Real You, you can notice where that energy is coming from, to transform and restore The Even Flow, and again come closer to The Real You.

Seeing Another For Who They Truly Are

Find a partner to do this with. Take your partner's hand or hands and really look at them and connect with them. If this is uncomfortable, soften flow and release that blocked energy you have until you can really become open and absorb their energy.

Reach with your sensors for their Creative Template, who they are when they are in total Even Flow. Hold eye contact. That's a lot of energy, soften and flow if you have to.

Feel what that energy is like, let it soften and flow through you. If you feel overwhelmed with any energy that you struggle to handle, breathe into that, soften flow and release. You will rejoice in what you see and experience. You may wish to let them know what you saw and felt. They may be living far from this potential and may be surprised to know about what is there for them to experience. Now you have something to help them work towards.

For the partner who is being seen and accepted in this deep way, this can also be an emotional experience. If your partner becomes emotional, direct them to breathe, soften and flow and release that pressure. Give them the time they need, then continue until they are happy to bask in your gaze as you rejoice in their splendour.

Contemplate for a moment the level of connection you have with this person, and your own feelings, and the beauty inherent in each person's spirit.

Then swap roles. Enjoy.

If you remember, think about this concept as you go about your daily life. The Real Spirit is within and behind the cloaks of what we present to each other in life.

Experiment with reading people's creative template energy, seeing what that feels like. It's a very pleasurable and joyful thing to do. As you brighten up with all that energy you are absorbing you can radiate some of that sparkle back out there.

CHAPTER 32

Loving Your Perfect Body

Our physical bodies are often neglected by so many of us. This is a topic that millions and millions struggle with. How we feel about our physical body explains why we cover up, why we wear make-up, often why we diet, why we over eat, why we under eat, why we need a six-pack and muscle definition, why we seek plastic surgery and botox, breast enlargement, breast reduction, tummy tucks, face lifts, nose jobs and stomach surgery. Who can blame us when our society is so obsessed with a particular definition of physical beauty? This is the beauty that is only skin deep.

What we are concerned with is inner beauty—the beauty of the spirit. When this shines strong from within, a person becomes beautiful even though their appearance may not fit society's conventions of beauty. They are radiant and confident and that energy is attractive. But for so many, their relationship with their physical body is not one of love, it is one of loathing. These negative emotions are energy disturbances in the energy system relating to physical appearance. These disturbances disrupt the Even Flow and stop us from loving ourselves completely. They stop us from being radiant and shiny and beautiful from within as we could be with the confidence and self esteem that this inner beauty brings.

Learning to love, accept and honour our physical bodies is a wondrous thing. Equally wondrous and holy is to help another human being to reach that state of self acceptance, self love and inner beauty. Creative genius, Silvia Hartmann, developed a beautiful ritual process to help us to heal the energy disturbances, the negative emotions we have about our physical body. I will share the exercises of how to do this with a partner. It's a most loving, exquisite, sacred ritual. You can do this for a friend or for your intimate partner. You can do it for your pets; they love it too! It will enrich any relationship and help the receiver to become more confident and accepting about themselves through deep nourishment and healing. It's called Beauty T. Silvia quite rightly offers this as a real alternative to cosmetic surgery. Changing your breast size might change your physical person, but your spirit person still has those injuries.

This process would be a great addition to all Beauty Salons, to be able to offer a Salon for Inner Beauty as well as outer beauty. Then clients really would emerge totally radiant! To seek out further training in how to offer this healing and nourishment to another person in the form of Beauty T, contact your nearest EmoTrance Trainer. But for now we can help a friend or have a friend help us in the following way.

Healing Specific Injuries

Is there a particular part of the body that you do not love and accept or consider to be perfect? For example, your nose, hair, stomach, thighs, breasts, genitals. It may be that your relationship with this part of your body has been damaged by childhood jibes or other traumatic events relating to that part of you. Whatever it is, ask yourself how you feel about that part of you? Then ask, where do you feel that in your body? Soften and flow until all the negative emotions are released.

Reconnecting Our Parts

Next we reconnect all our body parts. We have all these divisions: head, neck, wrists, neckline and breasts, waist, hips, genitals, ankles. Our clothes and accessories show up all these divisions about what is acceptable to show, and what is not. These divisions are also divisions in our spirit body energetic barriers disrupting free energy flow. This first exercises allows us to think of and reconnect the body as one whole body, as opposed to a collection of parts.

Both Exercise 18: Reconnecting Our Parts as One Body (page 126) and Exercise 19: Healing Our Relationship With Our Physical Body (page 128) are best done with a partner to facilitate for your maximum benefit. You can swap roles afterwards.

We have seen in this book how energy nutrition actually has a healing power in its own right. Taking in another energy from a person, from Source, an energy we might invoke such as water; whatever it is, this extra energy has the power to soften and dissolve energy disturbances and so is healing, and helps to restore the flow.

Exercise 19: Healing Our Relationship With Our Physical Body, is a powerful exercise to heal our dislike and loathing about different parts of our body by attending to each part and giving it some energy nutrition. What we use as energy nutrition is simply a statement of truth about that part. We can't say anything that could trigger self judgement, so we don't say "this beautiful nose," we just want something simple and true that will go in directly and easily to do its healing work. We remind ourselves that there is a Creative Order to all things. That we all come from this Creative Order and that all parts of us are designed by the same Creative Order, and therefore by definition, are beloved by the Creator. This way we are invoking the Love of Source to be received by our partner into each part of their body. The facilitator thus starts at the top, with the hair, and with permission from the receiver,

Reconnecting Our Parts as One Body

Do this exercise with a partner or EmoTrance Practitioner.

Important note to the facilitator for steps 1 and 2: Recognising that the receiver may have energy disturbances about different body parts, it is important that you yourself approach this process with a pure and open heart and without judgement. This way your energy will be more easily accepted by the receiver.

Step 1

Working from the head down towards the toe, make sweeping movements across the lines of division; e.g., sweeping from head through the neck to the shoulder saying "one body, your body."

Use a light touch on the receiver's body with these sweeping movements. This allows the receiver to focus on this part the body with the intention of reconnecting and restoring the flow by echoing "one body, my body."

Sweep down the arms, focusing on flowing the energy across the wrists through to the finger tips. Again say, "One body, your body." The receiver echoes "one body, my body" as he or she holds the intention of restoring flow and thinking of those parts as now one body.

Continue these long, light sweeping movements 2 to 3 times along each area, guiding the focus by saying, "One body, your body," while the receiver affirms, "one body, my body."

Step 2

Sweep down the receiver's back through the waist to the hips. Then sweep from the waist, across the bottom and down to the legs.

Sweep from the hips and down the legs to the feet. Sweep from the neck, through the chest, to the waist. Sweep from the waist, across the belly, over the genitals, and to the legs

Then make longer sweeping strokes from the top of the head all the way down to the feet at the front, back, and each side. Then, finally sweep down each side simultaneously from head to toe, then front and back simultaneously from head to toe, with the facilitator saying, "One body, your body," and the receiver affirming, "One body, my body."

The touch should be very light. Always ask permission when working with a partner saying, "Is it alright if I touch you or do you prefer that I hover over your body?"

The process can be done completely without actual contact, effectively stroking down the aura. It's a truly lovely, respectful thing to do for someone, and helps them to start to feel the wholeness about their physical body.

touches the hair lightly saying something like: "This is your hair, keeping your head warm, giving definition to your face, this hair is given to you by the Creative Order and is thus beloved." The facilitator takes their time. The receiver takes in that energy via that part of their body, softening and flowing to absorb and to get the benefit of that nourishment and to allow healing in the energy system to take place where there are injuries.

Again, it is very important that the facilitator does this in a loving non-judgmental way so that the energy is received easily. In fact as you continue to invoke the Creative Order in this ritual, a sacred energy develops to the whole process.

The receiver may become emotional at different parts of the body. It is important to pause at these parts and give the receiver the guidance and the time to breathe, soften and flow, and to release these old energies.

As the facilitator goes through the ritual, they also may become triggered while they put their attention to different parts of their partner's body. Again, soften and flow for your own healing and to keep the energy in flow for your partner.

Healing Our Relationship With Our Physical Body

Here's how the process might go with some suggestions for wording. The words need not be exact, they only need to be true. Adjust the words for a male receiver as appropriate. Pause between each section to allow the receiver time to absorb, to soften, and to flow.

Hair: This is your hair, covering your head, keeping it warm, thick and shiny, given to you by the Creative Order and therefore perfect and beloved.

Ears: These are your ears. They hear all the sounds of the earth: music, laughter, words of love, given to you by the Creative Order and so beloved.

Eyes: These are your eyes. They see the beauty of the world: colours, faces, nature, allowing you to express emotion, and to show your shining spirit to the world. Your eyes are given to you by the same Creative Order that made your hair and your ears and are therefore beloved.

Eyebrows: These are your eyebrows, framing your eyes, made by the same Creative Order, and also beloved.

Nose: This is your nose. It smells all the fragrances and perfumes of nature and food, allowing you to breathe in the breath of life. It is designed by the Creative Order and therefore beloved.

Mouth: This is your mouth with which you to speak and communicate, to taste food and drink, to kiss those you love. Given to you by the Creative Order, and therefore also beloved.

Head: This is your head, enclosing your brain, an amazing design, given to you by the Creative Order and so, beloved.

Neck: This is your neck, supporting your head, allowing you to turn and see around you. Given to you by the Creative Order, and therefore perfect and beloved.

Arms: These are your arms, working hard for you every day, allowing you to interact with life, allowing you to hug your loved ones, and given to you by the same Creative Order and thus beloved.

Hands: These are your hands and fingers that allow you to engage with life, to touch the world around you, to touch the ones you love, designed by the Creative Order and therefore beloved.

Spine: This is your spine, holding you upright, allowing you to bend and twist, working hard for you all day, given to you by the same Creative Order that made your eyes, hands, mouth ears, and therefore also beloved.

Breasts: (Women only) These are your breasts, part of your womanhood, allowing you to feed your young, adding curves to your body. There for the comfort of you and your loved ones, created by the Creative Order and therefore beloved.

Chest: This is your chest, protecting your heart and lungs and organs, given to you by the Creative Order and thus beloved.

Belly: This is your belly, containing your digestive system that allows you to derive nourishment, given to you by the Creative Order and so beloved.

Genitals: These are your genitals, allowing you to take part in the creation of new life, there for your pleasure, given to you by the same Creative Order that made your hands, your eyes, your mouth, your ears and is also therefore beloved.

Bottom: This is your bottom, fleshy or muscular, for sitting in comfort, for giving power to walking forward in life, given to you by the Creative Order and also beloved.

Legs: These are your legs, your hard-working legs, allowing you to go out into the world, given to you by the Creative Order and thus beloved.

Feet: These are your feet, taking you step by step through life, that allow you to dance, to walk, to run, to stand, given to you by the Creative Order and therefore beloved.

Whole Body: This is your body, given to you by the Creative Order and therefore beloved.

The words aren't as important as the intention and the time for the healing energy to be received and any softening and releasing to take place. If you are not easy in your expressiveness, keep it simple and true.

IMPORTANT NOTE

When attending to breasts and genital areas, hover your hands over those areas. Please bear in mind that different body parts will require more time to receive energy for healing and the energy of some body parts may be very emotional for the receiver as it triggers energetic injuries. Be prepared to hold your attention there and to guide the receiver to soften and flow as they take in that loving attention and truth and release that old energy.

If you are working with an intimate partner, this would be a very powerful exercise to do unclothed, as the process may be more emotionally challenging. There is, therefore, more opportunity for releasing greater emotional energy and so very much more rewarding in the resulting openness and freedom when the healing has taken place. This loving and honouring of the physical body of your partner can lead to a deeper spiritual intimacy as it allows greater spiritual openness and acceptance of the other person's energy and intentions.

A Self Help Version

Although much more powerful with a partner to facilitate, you could do this process for yourself, lying or sitting down, or in the bath or shower, taking each part of the body in turn and affirming its purpose and it's perfection and that it is beloved by the Creative Order. At each body part, take the time to absorb the loving intention given to that part of the body, soften and flow to really get the nourishment and healing available.

Contemplate the wonder and beauty of your physical body and notice how differently you feel towards it now.

CHAPTER 33

*I*ncreasing Your Sexual Energy

*W*e have already glimpsed in some of the stories of reconciled relationships, Sue and John earlier in this book and Amy and John in "His Stress Was Too Much For Me," page 165, how physical attraction diminished through stress (blocked energy) and how releasing the stress (restoring the flow), restored healthy physical desire.

These two examples were from the women's side. We can equally well explore what emotional issues may be going on the man's side, which diminish his desire and sexual function. Exploring what emotions are being experienced about the subject of physical intimacy, and restoring the energy flow, is often all that is needed.

For a recent client of mine, his performance in the bedroom with his new partner was shortened because of feelings of guilt arising from his love of his wife who had died. By assisting him to fully release the pain of the passing of his wife and these guilt feelings he was not only able to feel more confident and experience improvement in his physical relationship, but also more free to allow himself to become closer to his new girlfriend.

This next case was the client of a Urologist who uses transforming emotional energy techniques, EmoTrance and EFT with some of his patients.

Here's the story related by the Urologist:

> The client was a healthy 45-year-old man who was having some erectile dysfunction. He also knew that I do some mind-body work, and was hoping that I could help. I wondered if he was storing some old past trauma in his body, since keeping these traumas held deeply in the body uses up a huge amount of energy that could otherwise be used for healing, libido, or sexual function.
>
> He denied having any major childhood trauma, but mentioned in passing that his mother was an alcoholic. I asked him if there were any memories from his childhood that still held any emotional charge on them. He recounted the following memory, and as he told it to me, quite a bit of emotional intensity came up (8 on a scale of 0–10).
>
> His mother had been drinking all day, and he walked into the kitchen

to find his mother physically beating up his father, and hitting him with a heavy pan. The father left the house quite bloodied, came back a couple of hours later, packed up his stuff and left, never to return again, and never really having said "good bye" to the kids. As we focussed on the energy of this issue, we were able to remove all the emotional intensity. The specific aspects we focussed on were:

1. His abusive mother

2. The sense of abandonment when his father left: "How could he do this to me? He must not have loved us to be able to pick up and leave, then never contact us again, etc."

After our EmoTrance and EFT session, the client's wife went to work the following Monday with a huge smile on her face. She said that her husband had turned into a sexual animal. At one-month follow-up, his erections were still functioning fine without him needing to take any medication. And, the best part is that all of this took only about 10 minutes in the midst of a busy medical clinic." See Exercise 20: Restoring or Increasing Physical Desire (page 132), to experience this process.

Restoring or Increasing Physical Desire

The following approach could be helpful to release blocked energy which can be contributing to lack of desire or performance.

- When you think about physical intimacy with your partner, what do you feel in your body?

- Check outside your body for energy barriers as well as inside for blocked energy.

- To find an energy shield, imagine your partner approaching you with the intention of being physically intimate?

- Check how close they can approach before you become uncomfortable.

- Clear inner disturbances before releasing the shield in the gradual way we have learned so far.

Another way to deal with shields is to visualise the person approaching, clear the disturbance, then let them approach closer, clear any new disturbance. Continue in this way until all barriers or resistances to intimacy have been released.

- When all of the energy is released test.

- Think of physical intimacy and what that means to you again.

- Are there any remaining disturbances to clear?

Getting Energised

As a measure of your progress so far, score for yourself on a scale of 0 to 10, 10 being the strongest, on how strong the attraction and desire is right now.

Let's say it's now a 6. This then means there is still something blocking your desire from being 10?

Whatever your score, ask yourself, "Where do I feel that remaining resistance?"

Soften and Flow

Test again and repeat until you feel a 10 and your feelings of attraction and desire are restored.

IMPORTANT NOTE

For those who have had past trauma involving physical intimacy, the energetic injuries are quire severe and maybe complex. This is definitely an area which would benefit from the help of an experienced EmoTrance Practitioner.

Physical Intimacy

During physical intimacy you may become aware of other emotional issues that arise but that have not been addressed so far: fear of being seen, fear of letting go, fear of expressing yourself, anxiety about performance, etc.

With a considerate partner, you might ask your partner to allow you a moment to soften and release this energy, or you may take some time later, after your intimate time, to tune into that, soften and flow, so that it is released for the next time, thus enhancing your intimacy.

Emotional energy can also release via your partner. If you are able to express openly how you feel, and your partner can maintain a loving attention and accepting understanding of how you feel, this allows for your energy to release through your partner, deepening intimacy, understanding, and connection.

You may also enhance your physical experience by being aware of the sensations of energy building in your body, with the intention that they soften and flow more easily, thus increasing the extent of your physical experience.

Explore transforming emotional energy in your physical relationship. Explore simply how the sensations of your partners touch can be transformed into new experiences as the energy is allowed to flow more freely.

# aring to Love the Unlovable

That which is the greatest challenge holds within it the greatest gift for us

This is a very challenging topic and one that I recommend you explore for your own personal development when you are ready. When something or someone is unlovable by your judgement this is always because of strong shields and barriers, which indicate energetic injuries that we have behind those barriers, which we do not want to be triggered, as this causes us too much pain and discomfort. Or, our energy system is just not yet developed enough to handle certain energies, so those energy flowing through the young narrow channels and systems cause pressure and pain as the energy dams up. So again, it's safer not to allow it to enter at all.

This chapter is not for the faint hearted. It will challenge you. If you feel uncomfortable reading this section, notice where you feel this discomfort, soften and flow so that you may increase your understanding of the subject. You may dismiss this section completely. Know that these are your shields working to keep you from feeling any discomfort, which will also keep you from learning something new and potentially transforming. You are free to keep these shields. They are yours.

But remember: that which is the greatest challenge has within it the greatest gift for us.

The energies we are holding back behind those shields have much to bring us in learning, enrichment, compassion, healing, great love and wisdom. This is transformation and spiritual evolution. In the full unobstructed flow, from the deep knowledge and understanding that we gain from fully accepting this energy, we have absolute clarity and resources available to us that we didn't know existed and which we can direct towards peace, reconciliation, appropriate action and engagement. The more we understand, the better our decisions. The more we don't understand, the greater our ignorance, the more we can misjudge a situation, make bad decisions and opportunities for peace, healing and change are lost.

These strong barriers are the divisions in families, societies, religion, cultures, politics and internationally. When such strong shields and divisions exist there are consequences.

Consequences for the One with the Shields

Ignorance, lack of understanding, inaccurate judgement, a high risk of creating greater suffering from those we are disconnected from and a great lost opportunity. For the one with the shields it's a lost opportunity for spiritual evolution and development, and the greater opportunity for healing, transformation and reconciliation in those shielded out. Disconnection means numbness. This allows a person to act in ways that cause more injury and harm to others, as they are totally disconnected from the consequences of their actions. They feel nothing. It also perpetuates the status quo. Nothing changes. Stalemate. The problem persists.

A prominent politician recently said, "Sometimes you have to disconnect yourself from the consequences of your decisions as they are so enormous—otherwise you just couldn't take the decisions you need to do your job." That is exactly the reason why you must stay open and connected, so that you can feel the consequences of your actions. The more connection and flow, the more understanding, the more clarity, the more resources you have to take the appropriate action. But as you disconnect, you feel nothing of the damage that you may then cause. Our aim is not disconnection to feel nothing, it is reconnection, to engage the wisdom of the heart and increase our resourcefulness.

Consequences for Those Shielded Out

Those who are shielded out, exclude and misunderstood, vent their frustration at not being heard, their anger and rage at their pain being unacknowledged. This can be expressed in many ways. It may be with words; it may be with actions. What every human being needs is acceptance, understanding, recognition and appreciation. We have seen how this diffuses the emotional pressures allowing healing and transformation to take place. Shielding out and disconnecting only perpetuates the problem.

These energetic phenomena occur in many places in life. Let's consider some of the 'unlovables': bullies, killers, paedophiles, the enemy in war, criminals, abusers, religious fundamentalists, terrorists, certain politicians… I am sure that you can think of many, many more.

It's very interesting to observe that those 'unlovables' may also have become so disconnected that they act in this way that is unlovable to us.

Remember, words and actions arise from the energy state within.

Is the energy flowing or is it blocked? Are we happy or in pain?

Our behaviour is a reflection of our energy state.

If you are happy and feel love you act and speak from happiness and love. It is impossible to bully someone, to commit violence on a person or persons if you are in flow. To be able to act in this way a person can only be in so much anger pain and have so much fear or worse, have become so disconnected themselves as a result, that they can act freely in this way.

Two Mothers: Palestinian and Jewish

I was watching a TV documentary recently about two mothers, a Palestinian and a Jew. The Palestinian was the mother of a 17-year-old daughter and suicide bomber who caused the death of a 17-year-old Jewish girl at a shopping centre a few years ago. After some time, the Jewish mother wanted to talk to the Palestinian, mother to mother, to try to understand and make sense of the wasted young lives, and to create an opportunity for some kind of reconciliation—a public demonstration of the possibility of peace.

They met on video conference, and I watched while each 'said' they wanted peace. Neither was able to listen or understand the other's point of view. Each was disconnected and shielded to the real plight of the other. This complete refusal to listen, to accept, to understand each other, meant they were at a stalemate. The attempt failed.

I watched this with a fellow EmoTrance Trainer, while we were at our New York hotel for the USA EmoTrance launch in November. Both of us could see the energetics of what was happening, we could see what was needed and both of us could see HOW that could be achieved. One good thing about EmoTrance is that you start to look at life from the perspective of energy flow: how it is flowing and where it gets stuck. This makes it easy to see where a problem is and what we can do to solve it. Anyway, neither mother was emotionally ABLE to accept the other; they were strongly resistant to each other's plight. Willingness alone was not enough without some help. Until at least one side was able to accept the other's situation and feelings and to recognise and appreciate where they were coming from, the other would not be interested to listen or co-operate. Energy needs to flow; and everyone needs energy nutrition. Who starts first? The one who has the ability and understanding to do that; the bigger person—or else some facilitation is needed by someone who understands the principles of transformation of emotional energy.

We all know there is a desperate need for real healing in these parts of the world. Until these severe energetic injuries sustained during these times of conflict have been repaired, or until each can really listen and care about the plight of the other, until there is acknowledgement, recognition and appreciation of the other's position, there will continue to be pain, anger, resistance, defiance, desire for vengeance to inflict yet more harm. Aggression comes from a person with severe energetic injuries within.

But there is hope. People can learn how to transform this emotional energy, for healing, peace, clarity, and for the resources for peace and reconciliation. We need an army of educators and facilitators of healing and reconciliation for both sides. We need to transform the pain, the anger, the desire for vengeance into healing, acceptance of what has happened, wisdom, learning, and a different kind of resourcefulness which can be harnessed for peace.

Soldiers and Their Shields

I was reading an article about an army veteran becoming a conscientious objector after years in Iraq. The military refused to accept this and he is now in prison for misconduct. The officer's wife had the opportunity to talk to her husband's commanding officer and ask him had he killed people and did it not effect him when he saw the effects of his actions and what did he think about conscientious objection? He said, "We've got to teach these boys to shoot and look away, and they wouldn't be so bothered by what they did."[11]

Soldiers are trained to develop energetic shields and barriers and to dehumanise the 'enemy' so they can do their job of killing. This is the only way they can do it. To block out that this is someone's father, or brother, or son—a human being; and not to think about the trauma to that person's family who has to pick up the scattered body parts of their family member, to bury them, and to live with that pain. If it was their own family member, friend or neighbour, a person with a normal healthy functioning of their spirit person would not be able to act to harm someone in this way. It goes against human nature. Only with such strong shields could one human being be disconnected enough to inflict such an injury on another human being. Disconnection and how we act and speak from disconnection is the complete opposite of love. Love is complete connection and flow.

We are each free to choose who we want to be and what influence we want to have in the world. There are consequences of our choices, the waves of energy that go out into the world as a result of our actions.

When we drop our shields, to let life in, we can feel the results of our actions, restore our even flow, re-connect with our heart's wisdom and act from love in our life.

I have realised that this chapter is worth a whole book on Daring to Love the Unlovable, and what outcomes we might have in our world, if we could drop our shields and allow more of life and love in. That sounds like a great spiritual research project to me.

So how can we move towards flow, reconnection and love? By taking an aggressive, exclusive stance against such people? In other words, blocking them out? Refusing to engage and have dialogue? A bully is also a human being. A fundamentalist is also a human being. A soldier is also a human being. A politician is also a human being. How did they get to be the person they are living today? What happened to them? Unless we reach out, to engage, seek to understand divisions will continue to persist with the consequences that we know only too well.

Compassion is not weakness it is strength of spirit. Compassion brings clarity and with it resourcefulness. Righteous anger is still anger. And the resources available to a person in anger are less that those available to a person with the clarity of flow and understanding.

Could a willingness to reach out, engage, and understand the plight of others with openness, humanity, respect and appreciation for others move us towards healing and reconciliation even with 'unlovables'?

Remember, energy needs to flow and everyone needs energy nutrition. Exercise 21: Daring to Love the Unlovable, is not for the faint of heart or the weak in spirit. Do not attempt the later exercises until you feel ready having completed earlier exercises and having some skills and the desire to explore your own deeper spirituality. Do this with a partner who can help you with the energies you will have to handle. You have been warned. If you get into deep waters, get help from an EmoTrance Practitioner. And remember all emotion is only energy either blocked or flowing.

Here are a few more illustrations to show you that "it's all energy, only energy."

EmoTrancing A Killer

I was working with a new ET trainer who was happy to accept, soften and flow certain concepts and energies, but not others. I couldn't certify her as a trainer because she hadn't grasped the fundamental principle that "its all energy, and only energy;" her own judgement filters were getting in her way. So I asked her to EmoTrance something really, really challenging, which she would be very resistant to accepting. She chose the concept of a killer. She did work as a prison visitor and therapist and this was a concept she had encountered, but she refused to accept in any way.

So approaching this concept through her shield to it, starting with a tiny amount of this energy, she allowed it in. It hurt, it was disgusting, it was a thick treacly feeling inside; it made her feel sick. But we softened and flowed all of this, until she was ready to handle a bit more. Step by step we increasingly opened the shield allowing more energy in, through and out, repairing her energy injuries along the way until there was no shield and she could totally accept that energy with complete flow.

I asked her what did she get or learn from that. It was a profound moment.

There was along pause before she could speak then she slowly said "I don't know in my head, I don't know in my heart, but I know in my total being what that is about now. I know in my whole being how any person could have a set of life experiences, leaving such scars, such pain, such anger, such disconnection to lead them to such a place where they can commit such an act, even me, and that there, but for the grace of God, go I."

This was a great learning for her and for me.

Daring to Love the Unlovable

Warning: Risk of serious spiritual growth and learning with this exercise. The greater the challenge, the greater the gift within.

We have discussed a few of the common "Unlovables" such as: bullies, killers, paedophiles, enemies in war, criminals, abusers, religious fundamentalists, terrorists, certain politicians...I am sure that you can think of a few more.

Choose something that you are very strongly resistant to and work with a partner who has read the book or an EmoTrance friend or practitioner who knows how to work with shields.

Use the approach described in Exercise 8: Releasing Shields (page 57) to develop the ability to handle this energy bit by bit, repairing your energy system as you go. Remember previous **Energy Master Tips** for speeding up the process; e.g., introducing the energy of water into a resistant energy, or simply having the intention that its softening or releasing faster.

When you can handle all of that energy, contemplate and discuss what you learned and gained from it. Take it to the ultimate degree. Ask, "How much can I love that person now?"

Clear any more injuries and barriers to love. See if there are other ways you can help that person.

Tune into what experience(s) they may have had which gave rise to the energy state behind the actions they have committed. Ask, "Where do I feel this in my body?" Soften and flow and release.

Ask your Higher Self, or Divinity, "What can I offer this person?" Send that person an energy gift from you.

Note that by healing yourself to this extent, you are offering a path of release and thus helping that person towards healing by your love.

Experiment with other difficult concepts.

Notice any changes in your thinking, your attitude, in your resourcefulness, in your understanding and how you have changed as a person as a result. What have you learned about the nature of Love from this exercise?

Real learning takes place not only in our conscious mind, but in our totality. One who only takes information in on the level of the conscious mind, doesn't know in their heart, body and soul what that is about yet.

Energy Mastery Tip

Become aware of how you take in the energy of life and learning. Be open; allow that energy to flow through you. Notice the difference and the speed of learning when you do that for any subject. Notice how different your responses and resourcefulness are now compared to trying to analyse something completely in the conscious mind.

Now with that profound understanding and new clarity and her new resourcefulness and skills for engaging with such a person with the hope of some kind of transformation and rehabilitation, do you think there would be more chance or less chance for healing and transformation?

My Husband was a Paedophile

A client, Maureen, came to see me about her blood pressure and emotional stress and weight gain. We tracked her BP and weight gain back to a time 20 years earlier when she discovered that her husband had been abusing under-age boys in the park. It was a very traumatic revelation and was followed by period of great stress, leading to her weight gain. They eventually divorced. He spent time in custody. Our main aim was to release this entire old trauma from her system, and as a result she went on to lose a several stones in weight and her blood pressure came down. We had two sessions together, and at the end of this second session we explored how far she had come. She said that the idea of a paedophile was still very difficult for her. She was totally closed to it. She said she could watch a film that possibly included the themes, but a documentary about the subject she just couldn't watch as that would be too real.

Now having seen how she could release and transform emotional energy I invited her to explore this shield she had, as an experiment to see where it might lead and what she might get from that. So we approached a very strong shield to paedophiles in the step by step way, softening and flowing to develop her ability to handle this energy a bit at a time. At the end I asked her what got from that.

She said, "I actually can see now a human being with a lot of problems. I actually feel compassion. I would not have ever imagined I could experience that before." Many months later, speaking with Maureen, she said that dropping that final shield had allowed her to be a stronger person, and to be more trusting with men in her subsequent relationships; to be able to actually let someone in and accept help from them, which she couldn't do before. Maureen now has a happy relationship with a new partner. As for her ex-husband, he still had some problems, according to Maureen, but she herself had moved on.

We Are all Connected; We are All Responsible

We hear and read that we are all connected. That another person's pain is our pain. When one person injures another we are all injured; that we are all somehow responsible for each other. We have read this, but do we actually know this to be true in our own experience? Do we actually feel this? Why don't people feel this if it is true?

I have demonstrated in talking about relationship dynamics how one person can be a release channel for the blocked energy of another, if their heart is open and they are listening with love and can allow that energy in, through and out. I have also shared how in helping another who is not present, we can apply the same principle. By putting our attention somewhere, by having an open heart we can invite that energy in and see how it feels within us, soften and flow, and thereby create a change within the other person. So, in fact we are connected, not just to our family and loved ones. Simply by putting our attention somewhere we connect to that 'energy system' and if we are open, we can feel and release a problem in the person we are focussing upon.

The physics of this is explained in *The Field*, by Lynn McTaggart.

But for most people, we don't feel that connection. Our pathways are blocked, as we have seen, and some are completely shielded and disconnected. That's why we only feel connected to our close family and friends that we are open to. But let's return to being connected and explore that further. The fact that I can do this with my close family and friends means that in principle, I can do that with anyone if my heart channel is open and there is enough flow to handle what I then choose to put my attention on.

So given that our ability to accept, with love, another person's pain is a path of release and healing for that person and therefore the possibility for change, the converse is also true. Our inability to completely accept, flow and release a person's pain actually perpetuates the status quo. In other words, by NOT healing that within ourselves, which cannot handle another person's pain, we are perpetuating it. So we are complicit and responsible for the continuous pain and suffering that exists in the world simply by our blindness to it and our inability to handle it and so we recognise that we failed these people around us.

We may not have realised that until now, but we are, in this way, all responsible for each other.

So if we want and hope for change in the world; e.g. less violence and suffering, we have to change ourselves. We have to heal that within us that cannot accept, that within us that hurts, that judges, that despises, or that looks away in the face of the violence, suffering and pain. We need to develop our strong heart energy, to develop our strong energy flow, to build the flow of our compassion and love, not only to handle the suffering but to handle that which created the suffering.

Refusal to engage, blocking out, avoiding, threatening and overpowering will only help to perpetuate the problem. Energy needs to flow and everyone needs energy nutrition.

As we grow in our own love we grow in our ability to care. Only by caring enough will we engage and act for the release of suffering and prevention of aggression around us. As we heal ourselves, as we come closer to our Real Self, a flowing channel for the energy of love we can begin to care more, to acknowledge the real problems in the world around us and have the real desire and real ability to reach out and to help.

Healing the Dangerous and Mentally Ill in Hawaii

I recently heard about a Dr. Stanley Hew Len, who spent several years as a consulting clinical psychologist at the Hawaii State Hospital. He had profound results by using a healing process with the most dangerous and violent 'mentally ill' criminals in Hawaii. Yet he never talks to them, in fact, he never even sees them. He writes down their name and then just works on himself. He looks at their files and their history and he cleanses his own judgements, his own beliefs, his own attitudes and asks the Divinity what he can do for the person. For each incident in that person's history he say's "I am sorry, I love you, I love you." He is acknowledging his responsibility in having allowed that to happen, and giving total acceptance and love to the person for that act they committed or that experience they had. As he clears his own energy channels, pathways and injuries, and thereby healing himself, those attachments and memories are cleansed, and the patient improves.12,13 This is not legend. This is real. Dr Len has been working in this way for four years, with dramatic improvements to the patients in their mental and emotional state. Some were so improved they were allowed to go home. This is a work of great love and compassion, which can only grow stronger through this work over the years.

The cause of any problem is always blocked energy and energy needs to flow. By transforming emotional energy and restoring the flow we can create healing, understanding, and change in even more ways than we know.

This is an area that still challenges many of us, including me, and it is a work in progress in my own spiritual development. I ask myself how much I am doing to make a difference in the world around me. Basically, it comes down to "how much do I care?" I care to a degree, but feel my limitations. Like you, I am still facing new challenges, navigating my way through those energies for personal learning and transformation, in an effort to develop my capacity for love, to grow a stronger heart energy, to be able to handle more and to be able to make a bigger difference in the world around me.

"Father, forgive them, for they do not know what they do."
Luke 23:34 (Holy Bible)

CHAPTER 35

The X Factor Explained: How to Be a Star

I wanted to include this topic for love for a number of reasons. So many people are terrified of standing before any kind of audience and speaking, acting, singing, performing in any way. I was definitely one of them. This was my worst nightmare years ago. Here we have a situation when, let's say, the performer has some knowledge, art or passion about what they do and an opportunity to share that with many. There is thus the opportunity for the many to enjoy the performance—whatever it is—and for the performer to both love sharing his performance and absolutely be nourished and energized by the audience feedback and appreciation.

As a regular trainer working with groups, I have come to completely love what I do. I am so in flow with what I'm doing and can handle just about anything that could happen within that experience effortlessly. It's a real joy to be in that space and I gain so much personally from this exchange with groups of people. Yet years ago, I was the worst person you could imagine ever at public speaking. I had the worst phobia ever. So if anyone knows what's possible, I do!

Whether we are speaking or performing, we have similar fears and anxieties, and for sure now we know that "it's all energy, only energy" and that it can be softened and flowed away so we feel clear confident and relaxed.

When you are in flow; when you love your art and you love sharing that with others no matter the audience size, it's a wonderful energy high. How many young, up and coming musicians and stage performers have anxiety before they go on, and maybe even during their performance? So instead of having a few beers for Dutch courage before going on, how about releasing all that blocked energy so you can love all aspects of the show.

Exercise 22: Releasing the Passion for Performance (page 144), is for all public performers and speakers who know they have anxiety, yet who have passion for what they do and a desire to share it with others. *See also* "Audition Nerves: Panic to Passion," on page 175.

Releasing the Passion for Performance

Do this with an partner or ET Practitioner, or try it on your own. It's always nicer to work with a partner if you can find one. In Exercise 24: Assisting Another (page 151), I explain the energy benefits of working with another person. Remember, an ET Practitioner is only a phone call away.

Learn to love yourself and build a strong heart energy. Do Exercise 15: Heart Healing and Nutrition (page 116). Clear all blocks to your performance or art. Think about performing/speaking/acting/singing. What do you feel in your body? Soften and flow any energy disturbances

Connect With and Grow Your Passion

How passionate are you about what you do? (0 through 10) Where do you feel the passion? Soften and flow to see if you can make it flow more strongly. Clear all resistances until it's flowing really, really well.

Imagine standing in front of a small audience. They are looking at you and waiting. As you take in and receive their attention, what do you feel in your body? Check if there are any shields between you and the audience? If so, soften and bring that energy in and through a bit at a time. Clear all disturbances relating to handling their attention and expectations. Test until it's all flowing.

Now reconnect with or recall your passion for your art/subject as you imagine standing before your audience. Clear all disturbances until your passion is flowing again. Now visualise you are actually performing with your passion energy flowing. The audience is receiving this performance.

As you think of how it is being received, how do you feel in your body? Soften and flow disturbances to all kinds of receptions. Now imagine you are performing/speaking. How much do you love the situation you are in?

Clear all resistances to totally loving this situation. Make the affirmation: "I love performing for my audience." Clear all resistances/incongruences. Now absorb the audiences rapturous applause, in, through *and* out. Take it all in, let it really energize you and release it.

Options

Imagine a larger audience, go through the same steps. Imagine a sceptical closed audience, go through the same steps. Imagine you are waiting to go on next, soften and flow disturbances till you feel only excitement.

Test

Think of how you could test this in real life with a group of friends, at your next group meeting at work, or at your next rehearsal. Note the differences in your experience. If there are any new sensations, breathe, soften and flow as you feel them, or note what they are and deal with them again later.

When you become more relaxed in the live situation, consciously open to your audience and take their energy in, through and out. And make sure you do the same for your rapturous applause at the end.

CHAPTER 36

The Source and Power of Love

With our knowledge and skills for transforming emotional energy, this is a beautiful area where we can grow deeper in our relationship with our Source, the Divine, in whichever way we interpret it: God, Allah, The Creator, Jehovah or Universal Energy. We can even use EmoTrance principles to allow us to open up our heart channel and have new deeper and richer spiritual experience, simply by applying the same simple technique and principles.

Many years before EmoTrance I studied yoga, then later Christianity. I actually attended an Alpha course at my local church, learning more about Jesus; who he was and his teachings. There was a definite moment where I had a profound spiritual experience. I didn't understand what had happened back then, just accepted it for what it was but now I see energetically how it worked. Coming to understand Jesus as walking, talking, living, breathing Love, I came to a point of inviting Jesus into my life. I opened up and allowed his energy of Love in and through me. It was a deeply healing and moving experience. Everyone in the room could feel the energy that had descended on me. What I now understand was that I dropped my shields to unconditional Love and allowed that to flow in.

The spiritual awareness lasted some time, there was love and great joy in my life, but with time the feeling decreased in intensity. Life continued to happen, my channel started to get blocked with little things and then bigger things, until I felt spiritually dry and couldn't recapture that original experience again. I joined the church community for awhile; the prayer groups, which were wonderful, but church services didn't do it for me and the exclusiveness of the church and their 'apparent' insistence on them having monopoly on the truth turned me off. I didn't have the compassion or understanding at that time to see beyond the humanity and short-sightedness of individuals or to be able to accept and let go of the dogma. So I left to pursue my own path.

Later when I discovered about transforming emotional energy and EmoTrance, I now had new understanding of the energy behind different emotions, from fear to love. I had a way to let down my shields and barriers to let love in. I understood how to use my intention to create more flow within that I may begin to live in a more open-hearted way, engaging more fully in life, experiencing more happiness and joy.

I also learned how this same knowledge could be used to deepen my own relationship with my understanding of the Divine. As I prayed I was invoking the energy of the Divine, invoking the energy of Love and allowing that to flow in and through me now with a conscious understanding of what was happening keeping my connection to my Source open and flowing. Knowing that as life happens, and those energies build up and disrupt the flow of Source within me, I can understand what is happening, pay attention, soften and flow, and restore my relationship. So understanding about energy helped me in my Spiritual relationship.

Exercise 23: Deepening Your Spiritual Experience, shows you just a few ways that you might explore.

Washing Away Our 'Sins'?

Let's say our 'sins' arise from our negative emotional states; how we act and speak from those states. We understand well that these emotions are nothing more than energy blockages, disturbances and deficiencies in our energy body.

We have already seen how another energy introduced into our energy body where we have a disturbance, helps to soften the energy and to make it easier to flow and to release. You were invited to explore introducing the energy of water, with its dissolving properties, to assist in the Exercise 7: Handling Difficult Behaviours (page 49), and that works well.

We will also see in Chapter 37: Helping Someone Else With Their Love Problems (page 150), how another person's heart-felt desire and intention to help us has the effect of speeding up the softening and flowing and releasing of our energetic injuries, as demonstrated in the story of me singing to my friend and her burdens melting away in moments.

Maybe you have also experienced, as I have, the healing power of the energy of love, of another person. As we allow that to flow in, drinking that energy in, it can soften and release our energetic injuries.

From there it is only a small additional step to now understand how a powerful energy such as Divine Love, when we can be open enough and able enough to handle such a powerful energy, can result in massive healing, dissolving of energetic injuries old and new, releasing and transforming us. We can see now how a soul tormented can 'find God' and become a new person as old energetic injuries are simply washed away.

Connecting with Source Day to Day

My dear friend Margarita, who is a Catholic Sister, explained to me how she works with transforming the energy as she makes the sign of the Cross. She invokes

Deepening Your Spiritual Experience

Prayer

Choose a prayer that you like. I have chosen The Lord's Prayer as my example. Take each line one by one and take your time. As you say or think each line, contemplate the words and their qualities and meaning.

Feel the energy of those words. Notice where in your body you feel that. Put your attention there, think of the energy softening and flowing and allow those energies to flow deeper within, then through and out, then move on to the next line.

Remember, it is only in the releasing that the full transformation available from an energy takes place. If you hold onto it, you don't get the full value. Parts of your spirit remain as yet unnourished. Aim to let the energies flow in through and out.

The Lord's Prayer

Our Father in heaven,

hallowed be thy name.

Your Kingdom come,

your will be done,

on earth as in heaven

Give us today our daily bread.

Forgive us our sins,

as we forgive those who sin against us.

Lead us not into temptation,

but deliver us from evil.

For the kingdom, the power and the glory are yours.

Now and for ever. Amen

When you emerge from your prayer, contemplate the experience itself. Note any difference in the quality of your experience compared to your usual prayer.

Contemplate the energy dynamics of the prayer and what is being prayed for. "Our Father" is invoking Divine energy, "Your kingdom come" is inviting this energy into the real daily life, "our daily bread" is not just the food on the table its the energy food for our spirit. "Our sins" are the energy of guilt we hold for what we have said and done to another. With "those who sin against us," we are restoring the flow within our energy system. Forgiveness is letting go. "Deliver us from evil" is to release those disturbances within us, the blockages to love, which while there, can cause us to act and speak without love.

Exercise continued on next page

The following hymn is one of my favourites. You will appreciate now the energetic process at work in the first verse of this beautiful prayer by John Wimbler and how it encapsulates all that we have discussed about energy flow in, through and out, healing and releasing, restoring the flow of love. If you do not have a relationship with Jesus, you may wish to change the words to "Let the Breath of God enfold you."

Again, take it slowly, line by line, feel the energy of the words, feel that in your body, let the energy soften and flow through you and release, then take the next line. Afterwards, contemplate the depth of your experience.

> Let the Son of God enfold you
>
> With His Spirit and His Love
>
> Let Him fill your heart and satisfy your soul
>
> O let Him have the things that hold you
>
> And His Spirit like a dove
>
> Will descend upon your life and make you whole

Scripture

Whatever is your book of scripture, as you read, slow down, and contemplate the words. Feel the energy of the words in your body. If you are listening to recited verses, you also have the beautiful sounds and rhythms as well as the meaning and energy of the words. Soften and allow this energy to flow.

Contemplate your experience and how different it is, also your understanding or appreciation of the scripture you are working with.

There are many other ways you can use this understanding and awareness of energy flow to renew and to deepen your spiritual life, with God or with and through God's creation. Finding your shields and releasing them, releasing the build up of life energies which disrupt your connection, inviting in the oceans of energy around you, from all of Creation, invoking the energy of your Guru, your Prophet, and inviting his or her energy in. You are your own laboratory and there is much yet to explore.

the energies by naming them: "In the name of the Father and the Son and the Holy Spirit," and as she makes the sign of the Cross, she allows those energies to flow into her from above and down into her heart, then through her body, and out through her hands. In this way she brings Divine Love into the world through her life and actions on a daily basis.

Whether prayer is a regular ritual for you or it is anytime during the day, you can simply be more conscious of the energy you are invoking and connecting with, and of what's happening in your body as you invite those energies within.

When I think now of all those church services I attended in the past, I think about how much richer and nourishing they could have been for me, and for others, with understanding of how to transform emotional energy. There are so many opportunities during the prayers and rituals of the service to consciously work with the energies that are invoked, to be more open and allowing more flow and deeper nourishment. Attending funeral services we know is a time of great emotional pain and sadness for many in attendance. This is a huge opportunity for real healing and release, not in words, but in reality. Imagine if the leader of the service were to guide everyone in a meditation that allowed people to tune into their own pain in their hearts, to breathe into it, to allow it to soften. Or invoke the Love of God to enter each person, to allow time for injuries to soften and to release. So much of that energy of sadness could be transformed and released during the service.

There is certainly an opportunity for spiritual teachers to embrace these principles of transforming emotional energy, to seek out further learning, for the greater spiritual enrichment of the communities they serve.

When I set out to write this book, my aim was to write only of my direct experience personally and professionally, and therefore all that I shared would be absolutely true. Of organised religion I have had only a limited experience, and that limited experience was my introduction to Christianity. The principles of transforming emotional energy apply to humans in general, irrespective of their nationality or religious faith. It's about how we as a human being function spiritually in relation to our environment. The natural process of how we ingest, digest and eliminate energies and are transformed in the process is as natural a function as the way we process food, and is completely free of religious dogma. But as it's just a part of our self understanding, we can apply this understanding to deepening our relationships in ANY aspect of our life, including our Spirituality or Religious Faith.

So though I have used some Christian examples, the same principles apply for a person of any religion who wishes to deepen their spiritual experience.

CHAPTER 37

Helping Someone Else With Their Love Problems

During the earlier exercises you have experienced how you can transform your own emotional energy simply by being aware of where the disturbance comes from and having the intention for it to soften and to restore the Even Flow. So we are using the power of your intention to soften the energy.

Having a person assist you to release the same energy is more powerful in a number of ways. Firstly, we now have two people's intention directed to the energy disturbance to help it soften. Secondly, the open loving acceptance that the facilitator holds for you and your emotional state helps the energy to release, partly through the facilitator. Thirdly, the facilitator, with your permission, may also use their hands, hovering or with contact over the energy disturbance, and this adds another energy to assist in the softening. Fourthly, the greater the energy flow and state of the facilitator, the more energy they have to direct towards your healing.

So, if your facilitator is feeling flat, low, and disconnected themselves, there is some energy available to direct towards the subject's energy disturbance. But if the facilitator's energy is flowing well, they feel love and are energised then they have more energy available to pour into the subject to assist in the healing.

In many healing traditions, therapists are taught to protect themselves from their client's energies, with energy devices such as a 'cloak of protection' or 'energy barrier' of some kind. This is a coping mechanism for the therapist, which allows them to work to a degree with their client without being affected by their client. This is not how an EmoTrance Practitioner or facilitator works. Any energetic barrier is a barrier to energy flow, and energy needs to flow. The greater the openness, the greater capacity for flow within the facilitator, and the greater the opportunity for release within the client.

While facilitating or assisting healing for another person, if we do find that a client's problems or situation is a lot for us to handle, and triggers our own emotions, thus reducing our ability to be effective, the energetically optimum way is to notice that we have now found a type of energy that we need to do some work on, to be able to handle it better. This means that each person we assist actually becomes an opportunity for our own personal and spiritual growth. Exercise 24: Assisting Another, details ways in which you can help another heal themselves.

Assisting Another

Two intentions are better than one.

Ask your partner if they have an issue or problem they would like to resolve, or something they would like to change or release to make them feel happier.

- Ask them, "Where do you feel this in your body, show me with your hands."

- Tell them, "It's all energy, only energy, and energy responds to thought."

- Tell them, "You are going to work from the inside and I am going to work from the outside and together we are going to soften and to flow this energy to see where it can release."

- Tell them, "Focus on this energy and think of it softening and flowing."

- Tell them, "When its soft enough to flow, let me know which way it wants to go."

- You both do the same, holding your attention in the same place thinking, "Soften and flow."

- Ask them, "Tell me what's happening."

- You both follow the energy until it has released through and out of the body.

- You use your hands to follow the energy.

- You ask your partner, "Does it help you more if I place my hands here over the energy? Or does it help more if I hover my hands here?"

- Work it out together to discover what is best for the recipient.

- When all is released, go back and test

- Ask them, "Think of the problem again, how does it feel? Do we have anything remaining to clear?"

- Together, focus on the remaining energy, until its all softened, flowed and released.

- You test creatively until the recipient now feels more energised.

Exercise continued on next page

Important Note on Touching

Always ask permission of your partner before you touch them. When energy is travelling through or stuck in sexual areas, always hover at a respectful distance, checking out how comfortable it is for your partner. Energetic injuries in the neck area also require sensitivity. Hovering hands are more helpful here.

Question: I've not done any healing before. Do you have to use your hands?

If you feel awkward about using your hands to assist, as I was when I first started energy work, that's OK. It helps but is not necessary. You can have the intention of using your hands, imagining they are there hovering over the energy. This intention also works.

If you are helping a person by phone, clearly you can't work with them physically, but you can still use your intention along with your friend's and together you can soften and release the energy disturbance. You can increase the effectiveness by having the intention that your hands are hovering over that energy disturbance too, even though they are far away.

Question: How does intention work?

Thought is energy. Our energy body and its injuries are energy. Energy influences energy immediately. Intention is energy transmitted. Energy flows through the energy field through which we are all connected. You can read more about the science or physics of how intention works in Lynn McTaggart's excellent books *The Field* and follow-up book *The Intention Experiment*.

All we need to know is that where you put your attention, you connect to that energy system which you are focusing upon. Then when you hold your intention for an outcome, such as "the energy is softening" then energy is transferred to that place where your attention is focussed and influences the energetic system there in the way that you intend.

You can increase the power of your intention; i.e., increase the amount of energy transferred by increasing your own energy flow state. Hence the healing power of love and prayer. Notice also that as you hold a particular intention, your energy flows much stronger from your hands.

An EmoTrance Practitioner is therefore a human being with an open heart, and a heart-felt desire to assist another human being. They work together to soften and release an energetic injury and to restore flow.

The facilitator works from clear direct feedback from the 'client' about where the injury is, and what it feels like and where it wants to flow when the energy softens enough. They work together until all the energy is released, one asking for feedback and giving guidance and then both together holding the intention for the energy to soften and release, then again more feedback to check on progress. A facilitator, with permission from their partner, may use their hands hovering or touching the area which needs healing. The ;client' alone knows when the healing is done as they feel so much better, lighter and brighter. It's really so easy.

We don't have fancy maps of energy systems, we don't have complex procedures to follow. We don't have to train for years to learn this. It's easy. In fact it only takes two days to train to become a practitioner of EmoTrance.

Qualifications Needed to Assist Another

All you need as qualifications to assist another are:

- ↣ The understanding of energy flow and energy nutrition principles

- ↣ To have experienced the restoring of flow within yourself, so that you know what it feels like and what changes occur when the energy flow is restored

- ↣ To know the basic process:

  - Asking what the problem is

  - Asking "Where do you feel that in your body? Show me with your hands."

  - To know that it's all energy, only energy, and that our intention influences energy immediately, and to remind our partner about this

  - To guide your partner to think "soften and flow' and ask where the energy now wants to go, and for you to do the same

  - To ask for feedback about what's happening for our partner

  - To follow the energy through the body until it reaches an outlet and we allow it to release

  - To test and help the person ensure that all the energy has released and they are now feeling relaxed or energised

- ↣ To have the desire and intention to want to help another person

It is a beautiful joint healing process; a healing dance between two people. It's elegant in its simplicity; it's natural and almost anyone can do it.

EmoTrance Practitioner Training gives you the space to practice the energy transforming exercises and gain the learning and experience you need, and the opportunity to have your questions answered and to learn from the diverse experiences of a group. It also gives you the chance to develop the Energy Mastery Skills to speed the process up when energy is slow to release or gets stuck along the way so you can assist with deeper or more complex energetic injuries.

But you have the basics to help yourself and to assist a friend with what you have learned in this book if you have done some of the exercises and this will bring you great personal reward. When you assist someone to release an injury and to now feel so much brighter and lighter and happy again, you also derive the benefit of taking this bright energy in and deriving the nourishment from that. Assisting another in healing and transformation is a joy in itself and as a service to those around us informally or professionally, it is hard to find something to beat it in real heart-warming, satisfying work. It satisfies the soul. Becoming a Practitioner of EmoTrance for transforming emotional energy is such a rewarding work. You are helping another to heal their energy system, their energy body, their spirit. You helping to create lighter and brighter spirits in the world who can be more open, engage more fully in life and love. You help to change the world in which we live to be a better place.

Work that Satisfies the Soul

When I reflect on my life experiences, the ones I cherish the most or have touched me the deepest are always the ones which engaged my heart and spirit the most fully, which is why I love doing this kind of work. It's a joy. Not only through my clients, but as I go out in the world, with knowledge and understanding of energy flow and energy nutrition, my interactions with people are more rewarding in so many ways.

Live workshops create more opportunities for learning and allow you to meet new like-minded friends, some of whom will become your great ET buddies through your life. Imagine a world full of people who understood how to transform emotional energy for themselves and for others around them, at home, work and play, becoming a great influence for healing, for love and for peace and understanding in the world.

The world definitely needs more EmoTrance Practitioners so I invite you to join us, the growing international family of people who know how to transform emotional energy to create more lightness and love in the world.

See Additional Resources (page 191), for more details on workshops and training.

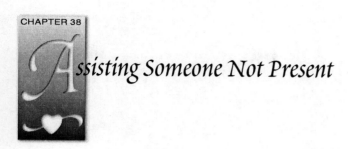

ssisting Someone Not Present

*I*f the person you want to help can't be beside you, you can easily work with them on the telephone. Just do it and see how well it works—bearing in mind that getting clear feedback about what's going on in your partner's energy system is important.

There are other ways that you can work. I mentioned while relating about my brother-in-law's death, how I helped my niece and nephew to handle some of what they were going through and it helped to release something for them, which allowed their behaviour to change. Remember also Dr Len in Hawaii, and his work of great love.

This is where you are consciously using your own energy system as a pathway for release of another person's energy. Example, my niece was feeling insecure about her mum going out. She was crying and being clingy and not wanting to go to school or be separated from her mum.

I tuned in to my niece's energy simply by opening my heart and asking: where do I feel her anxiety about also losing her mum in my body? Instantly I felt it as an emotional pain in my heart. I breathed, softened and flowed and released it. My niece became less anxious about going to school or about her mum going out. She had a release of an energetic injury; I gained an increase in capacity to handle another person's painful experience; i.e. greater compassion.

We can do this as and when the opportunity arises. We can also take some time during our quiet time prayer or meditation time, to do absent healing in this way, on our own or in a group, which multiplies the power of the healing intention.

Recognise here that our ability to be open, to accept and to handle another person's stress, is a path way for its release and thus assisting their healing, that as we heal ourselves we allow others to heal. Being equally stressed or feeling the pain when a friend is upset, doesn't help them as much since one path for the possible release of their energy is blocked.

CHAPTER 39

The Power of Another Person's Energy

One day my ET Buddy, Baya, called me in distress. Everything was getting on top of her; she was feeling overwhelmed and not able to cope. She felt pressure on her shoulders and back, it was heavy, it was hurting and she needed reassurance. She just wanted someone to tell her everything was going to be ok and that she was great and was able to cope.

Singing Baya's Problems Away

I directed her to focus on the hard heavy energy in her shoulders and started to give her the energy nutrients she needed telling her "you are amazing, you are wonderful. You are a bright shining star." The energy slowly started to soften. Then because my own energy was so good and I was so happy in myself that day, on impulse I started to sing it to her instead! The tune was a bit like, "I'm a Yankee Doodle Dandy... born on the 4th of July..." Yes, I have watched a lot of old Broadway musicals in my life! My words went something like:

> You are totally amazing,
> You are such a shining star.
> You're so totally amazing,
> Do you know how wonderful you are?
> You are totally amazing,
> You are such a shining star.
> Do you know how totally amazing?
> Do you know? We all know.
> Do you know? We all know.
> Yes we know just how wonderful you aaaaaare!

There was a whole orchestra and Broadway chorus going on in my head and the results were amazing. In the time it took to sing those few lines with joy and love and fun to my friend, 98 percent of that heavy energy had completely melted away. Yes, Baya knew how to be open and allow that energy in, soaking it up and letting it flow, so it worked well. But other times, we might have spent 10 whole minutes or more releasing all that same heaviness in the shoulders. I basically poured my energy into my friend and she was able to take it in, and let it do its magic. All her hard energy released so fast, we were both amazed and delighted, and it was a lovely and joyful healing experience that we shared.

Now I'm not saying you have to sing to all your friends! Although, that in itself would be so nice! I'm only sharing a spontaneous creative way that I used my intention more powerfully on one occasion. The main point is that the greater your own energy flow and state, the more powerful your intention for healing another will be. And we have the power to create the energy states within that increase our healing power. For example, try the affirmation "I am the perfect person to help this person in front of me right now" or "I am a great healer" and soften and release away all your resistances to that being true.

The best way to learn is to experiment yourself. You are your own energy laboratory.

CHAPTER 40

*S*uccess Through Love

*S*o far we have focused on our relationship with our partner and with our selves, and we have discovered how we can transform emotional energy into energy flow states and positive emotions. The very same principles apply literally in ALL aspects of life.

We have relationships with our work, pets, families, community, art, sport, musical performance, study, and more. Be it romance, marriage, family, schools, business, society, religion, politics, international relations, the whole world is energy flow and thus the whole world runs on emotion. (Emotion = Energy in motion.) When energy is flowing, we get the positive emotions and life flows smoothly. When energy is blocked we get negative emotions and... problems. You could write a book "Transforming Emotional Energy in..." and apply these principles in every aspect of life.

All life's problems arise when energy is blocked. So having the ability to transform emotional energy applies in every single endeavour. We say, "Everything works better with EmoTrance." Everything works better when the energy is flowing.

You can develop a Love relationship with just about anything. To demonstrate this point, I had a woman in a workshop who detested paperwork. She did everything to avoid it and was forever procrastinating about doing it. We first released all her negative emotions so she was neutral to it and didn't have anything against it, but I took her further to raise her energy until she was laughing incredulously that she actually now LOVED paperwork and admin and she literally was now excited and couldn't wait to get home to do it! Love is full flow energising and enriching and transforming us, giving us clarity and full resources to tackle whatever that area is. Imagine what you could achieve if you could create a flow state of LOVE for whatever you wanted to do. And now, you know how to do that.

You know how to identify where the energetic injuries or blockages are. You know how to use your intention to influence that energy to soften and restore the flow. You know how to reconnect in areas where you are disconnected and shielded for greater learning, and personal transformation. You now have the tools to create more love in all the aspects of your life that you desire. All you need now is to practice, to apply the knowledge in your daily life.

Sometimes it will be 'in the moment' when you feel an emotional response to something, and you can attend to that energy, restoring its flow as life happens.

Sometimes you will take time out to do some energy repairs later so that this area of your life flows and relationships more easily next time.

Sometimes you will find yourself face to face with another person in distress, on a boat, on a plane, at a party, out and about and you will have the understanding and ability to intervene and help that person to release the pressure a little, and to have brightened and made a real difference to their lives.

Some of you my now see a way that you can even help those who resist your help or who have difficulties interacting with you, by healing yourself and letting yourself be the channel towards their healing.

Some of you may be able to see how easily EmoTrance can integrate into skills you already have in working with people for healing and coaching and personal development.

Some of you maybe so drawn to this whole subject that you see a whole new rewarding way of working professionally and serving others in life by assisting people to restore the Even Flow and to help them along the way to becoming the person they were meant to be, to experience the life they were meant to live. I have a vision of walking, talking, living, breathing Love Clinics sprouting up all over the world, assisting people around them to create more love in their lives.

Whichever way you integrate this knowledge it will positively change you; it will positively change your life and it will cause positive change in the people around you.

CHAPTER 41

*T*owards a Future Filled With Love

*C*ongratulations to you on arriving this far. You have been on a journey through this book, especially if you have been putting these principles into practice. You will have already seen changes within yourself, in your relationships, and may have already begun to help others to do the same.

We have introduced fundamental principles of energy:

- ᙣ That energy needs to flow;

- ᙣ That we are spirit beings with an energy mind, energy heart, energy digestive system, energy hands and more;

- ᙣ That our spirit, or energy person, needs a constant flow of a variety of energy nutrients through us daily just as our physical body requires food;

- ᙣ That our emotions are nothing more than a reflection of the state of our energy system;

- ᙣ That blocked energy states cause us to experience negative emotions;

- ᙣ That simply by noticing and paying attention to where the energetic injury is, with our intention we can restore the flow;

- ᙣ That restoring the flow returns us to our natural state of being, The Even Flow;

- ᙣ That flow states in our energy body cause us to experience and enjoy positive emotions;

- ᙣ That transformation and learning takes place only when the energy has flowed in through and out, i.e. has been properly digested, assimilated and then released;

- ᙣ That there are no good or bad energies, its all energy and only energy;

- ᙣ That the way we handle it within our spirit body only determines whether that hurts us or nourishes us deeply;

～ That which is the greatest challenge has within it the greatest gift for us. The bigger the energy, the more potential there is for our learning and transformation when we can handle it completely, in, through and out. It's all energy, only energy;

～ We are designed as spiritual beings to handle and derive nourishment and benefit from all the energies that life brings us; and

～ That when we do handle well the energies of life we live the life we were designed to live. We experience the joy, love and success we were designed to experience. We discover our real potential.

Transforming **emo**tional energy—EmoTrance—is not a one-off solution to heal all your problems once and for all; it's a way of life. Whatever we heal today, life can present us something else even bigger to handle tomorrow. Understanding the flow of energy and living energy in our life we navigate the oceans of energy and ride its waves.

By transforming emotional energy pain turns to joy, judgement to understanding and compassion, ignorance to clarity, fear to courage. We open to the energies of life, life enriches us, we feel more love, we come closer to our true self and so the flow of life goes on.

The person that once sent out angry words and actions into the world is transformed into the happy loving person sending out happiness and love into the world.

The more flow we create for ourselves, the more joy happiness and love, and the more loving acts and words that go out into our relationships, our families, our work, our communities and the world around us. We can say, "I haven't got the time" or "It's too hard," or "I just can't handle that," or "There's too much to heal—I can't do it." Know that these are your limitations. We can now say: "And where do I feel that in my body?" then soften and restore the flow and move closer to creating a life without those limits—a life open to new possibilities. Or we can stay as we are, living our life as we are today. We have choice. Each is acceptable and each has its consequences not only for our self but for those around us. But now, we have both knowledge and the tools as we know that it's all energy, only energy, including those limitations, and that we really can choose the path towards greater love in our lives and the world around us. The question is now simply, "Who do you want to be?" You can stay as the person you are living out today with all the consequences of that or transform to become closer to The Real You, your true self and all the new possibilities that are just waiting for you to open to them. It's your choice.

By changing ourselves, we become the change that the world needs.

And what the world needs is more love.

Thanks to EmoTrance and my ET buddies I have been able to write this book in only a few weeks, but it is the work of my own exploration transforming emotional energy since EmoTrance was born in 2002. I have come along way since that sceptical beginning, thinking I was in a room full of weirdos with energy flowing out of their ears hands and feet, when I couldn't feel a thing, due to the shields that I didn't even know I had back then!

I hope this book and the additional stories that follow have been some inspiration to you; some food for thought and have provided you with the means to change your outlook, yourself, your life and relationships in some way for the better, and to take a step—or even a leap—forward. If it has, or if it hasn't I am both honoured and grateful to have been given the opportunity to make a difference.

Wishing you the real joy of living energy in your life.

May you come to know even greater love and happiness.

Thank you for reading.

Sandra Hillawi
11 December 2007

Inspiring Stories
of Healing and Love

ore Stories of Love and Healing

*T*he following stories are true stories submitted by EmoTrance Practitioners. To respect confidentiality where requested, names have been changed. The stories illustrate how, by transforming emotional energy, amazing transformation is available to us. I hope that you find them inspiring. Dip in and out or read them all.

His Stress was Too Much for Me

Amy had left her relationship six weeks earlier, after being with John for six months. It was over. John had been under a lot of stress at work and this had put a real strain on their relationship. After a very difficult period, with a lot of hurt and lack of consideration, Amy decided to leave as she could no longer cope with John's attitude and all physical attraction and desire on Amy's part had completely vanished. She new this was a pattern in her, running away when she couldn't cope any longer, but what else could she do? Here's how the session went.

Sandra: So when you think about John's behaviour to you, where do you feel this in your body?

Amy: In my stomach, like a heavy round pressure.

Sandra guides Amy with EmoTrance technique to soften this energy.

Amy: It's spreading out and seems to be flowing downwards to my hips and legs.

Sandra: Where does it want to go next, this energy?

Amy: I feel warmth travelling down my legs and my feet now feel heavy.

The energy finally leaves from the toes.

Sandra: So now, when you think about John's behaviour to you, how does it feel?

Amy: It's not so bad, but I still feel a small pressure in the stomach.

Sandra guides Amy as before and the energy travels down the legs and leaves the body again.

Amy: It's ok now, it's like, he can be stressed and I can see that he's not getting at me personally, he's just frustrated with his own issues. It doesn't affect me any more; it just makes me feel I want to support him. I can handle it.

Sandra: So what else bothers you about John?

We go through all the things that caused Amy to split up from John and apply the same process to locate the energy in the body, soften the energy and watch it flow and release from the body, until there was nothing else about John that Amy could find fault with. Then we turned to the physical relationship.

Sandra: So how much are you attracted to John at the moment? 0 to 10?

Amy: 0 at the moment.

Sandra: So when you think of being intimate with him, where do you feel this in your body?

Amy: In my chest, it's like a barrier.

We soften the energy again so that it flows and releases from the body, this time upwards and out through the mouth with the breath.

Sandra: So how much are you attracted to him now?

Amy: 3 out of 10.

Sandra: So there's still a big part of you that isn't attracted to him. Where do you feel this resistance?

Amy: Low down.

Sandra: So let's soften this energy too. Tell me when it's all released... Now how strong is your attraction?

Amy: 9 out of 10, (looking surprised and very pleased).

Sandra: So there's a tiny bit of you somewhere that doesn't desire him completely, where is that?

Amy: It feels like it's in my head actually, kind of near the side of my forehead.

We soften and release this energy and as you can imagine, we get to 10 out of 10 on desire and end up with a very happy Amy (not to mention a happy John) as the couple were subsequently reunited.

The exchange between us took place as a relaxed conversation during a leisurely sail down a river. No other passengers were aware of it; it was as if we were just having a chat. It's just so easy to help another in distress when you are out and about in the world.

A Happy Ending

Amy fell in love all over again with John. They reunited and are deeply in love. They moved in together and their relationship and intimacy is also happily restored.

Amy's relationship is flourishing, but it could have been over. Amy could have let this relationship go because she was not able to handle what life was presenting her at the time. By restoring flow in her own energy system not only did she strengthen and increase her ability to handle difficult behaviours, but at the same time, she could see them for what they were. What was a personal attack and inconsiderate behaviour now was just an expression of frustration in her partner and a need for her understanding and support, which, once cleared in herself she then had the resources to give.

The Love of My Life Found the Love of His Life...

...but it wasn't me! I'd had a relationship that drifted into being just friends, even after that I had still hoped that one day he would discover that he did love me and we would be reconciled. There was love, but it was platonic from his side. One day I received a phone call from my elated friend. "I just wanted to share with you as my good friend my news. At last I've found the love of my life, and I'm so happy." It hit me right in the chest 'BAM' and a welling up of emotion. I pretended to share in his happiness and when I finally ended the call, I only felt sadness and hurt, with hot energy filling my chest area and heat flushing into my face.

Knowing about transforming emotional energy I said to myself, "Right, it's only energy; soften and flow'. Miraculously for me the energy released up and out through my head. It completely released from my chest leaving such lightness and creating such a flow, which I could only describe as love once more restored. I smiled and laughed, yes I did love my dear friend and now I could also be truly happy for him. It all happened in a moment, the pain and sadness transformed to love and happiness in seconds.

The Angry Waiter Made My Day

I was having lunch at a café during the break on my EmoTrance workshop. I had reason to call the waiter over and ask to change the side salad as it looked a bit limp and old. He made a slightly sarcastic comment and gave me a look of 'hmmph, fussy customer,' which I felt really indignant about, until I noticed that I could feel my anger in my chest and throat. So, opportunity to practice? I softened and flowed and it wizzed up and out of my head, leaving me laughing in a moment of delight! I now felt uplifted and all thanks to that waiter who was obviously having a bad day himself! Wow, energy transformation in action...this really works!

The Stalker Brought Me Strength and Backbone

A girl came to me for help. She was scared because she was being stalked. It felt like a slimy scary energy that she didn't want to feel. The way she managed to cope knowing the stalker was around was to harden herself to this feeling of him in her life. She said it was like she had a shell of protection around her, keeping him out.

I asked her if she could make just a microscopic hole in the shield, just at the end of her little finger, to allow a tiny bit of that energy in, to see what it was like. There was great resistance that we had to clear before she was ready to do that. She let a tiny bit enter; the energy flowed up into her little finger.

I asked her how it felt. "Strange,", she said, "it's strengthened my little finger.". So she let that tiny thread of energy find its way through her body and out, and we cleared the resistances in her body along the way. Then increasingly bit by bit allowed more and more energy flow in and spread through her body, through her bones. At the end, when she felt energised, she said she felt that now she had strength and backbone for the first time in her life. The stalker stopped stalking.

This was one of the earlier EmoTrance sessions when EmoTrance was in its experimental stages. The results were surprising to us, but that is in fact exactly what happened.

I Couldn't Say 'I Love You' to My Dad

It was at the EmoTrance launch when I discovered that I had shields. I didn't feel much; I was always a stable and independent person. I didn't have successful long-term relationships. They went wrong when I used to get needy and then my boyfriends would withdraw. That made it worse and so the pattern went. I was an addictive kind of person, with food and in relationships. But I didn't see myself as having emotional problems really. Nothing really touched me, literally, because it couldn't get in!

Our family life was stable and secure, but we showed love for each other through actions, not through words. We weren't very tactile family—except with the kids. When I saw films on TV with adoring daughters and hugging their loving fathers I thought that's just Hollywood; it's not like that I real life, not in mine. The idea of hugging my dad made me cringe.

So at the conference when we learned about shields, I decided to explore my family relationships to see if I had any. I thought of a loving connection with each of them one by one, checking out how I felt. First my mum: I opened my heart by thinking of a loving connection with her—yes, that was ok. It felt like there was room for improvement, but it was a nice connection. Next my dad: I opened up to him and instantly closed again. I cringed and shuddered. Wow. What was that about? I had no idea that existed. So I had a shield to my dad.

After the training I couldn't wait to get to work on releasing this shield. With the help of my friend Kath, who came with me, we used the approach we had been taught: locate the shield, make a small hole in it, let a little energy in through and out, healing the energy disturbances along the way, then increasing the energy flow gradually till I could handle it all.

I had a lot of resistance to even starting the process, in my chest. We cleared it—most of it. There was a tiny bit left and I was too eager to get on with the actual shield so we left that tiny disturbance there and continued. I mention it now, as it became relevant a few weeks later.

So gradually I was able to handle my dad's energy. In fact, it was his love that I was holding back. As we progressed by letting down the shield, I became aware of a stronger and stronger flow of love in my body. In fact my initial thoughts were of fullness, which I'd never felt before.

The next day, I asked my dad round for a talk about our relationship. I was able to speak open-heartedly to him. It was emotional. We both hugged and I said, "I love you, Dad," and was aware that I couldn't remember being able to say that to him before. But I truly felt it now.

Our relationship was so much better. Now we had the hugs, affection and warmth I saw on TV. Now I understood. But that wasn't all—other things changed. I started to be able to leave things on my plate, instead of having to eat everything. I was full already before I finished my meal. I stopped chasing after men, and they started to chase after me. It was great!

A few weeks later, something happened and my barriers went up again. It was a certain behaviour that my dad did, which I judged to be unacceptable. It was interesting to observe myself return to deficiency again. In another two to three weeks I was back in my old eating habits and our relationship became more distant.

How come? Remember the preparation we did before letting the shield down? Well, it wasn't thorough. We'd left an energy disturbance about something, and this had been retriggered by his behaviour. The shield went back up and the energy nourishment I was getting stopped, so my old behaviours returned.

So how is my relationship now a few years later? Well it could be better. Since then other major things have happened, which I have yet to release in order to open up to him again at that level. It's a case of making the time and priority for it. Writing this is already motivating me to attend to that now… I feel another session coming on!

Thirty-Year Problem Released in a Phone Call

Just a day or two after I had read part of the EmoTrance book for the first time I called an associate—let's call her Ella—on the phone to discuss some details of a seminar I had given in her town. I immediately sensed that she wasn't alright and so I asked her if anything was wrong. Upon that question she burst into tears over problems in her family, people always interrupting her or even walking away while she was talking to them. She felt full of sadness and frustration. And for many, many years already these feeling had stood between her and her loved ones; between her and her friends.

After a few moments I heard myself ask her (I had not intended this consciously) whether she was willing to make a small experiment and try to relieve that pressure. She seemed slightly surprised, but she agreed.

So I asked her, "Where do you feel this in your body?" It was in her chest, near the heart, if I remember correctly. I let her put her hand there and soften that energy and I guided her letting it flow through and out of her body. The energy moved without any resistance and Ella felt transformations almost instantly.

It took us maybe 15–20 minutes to move all of the energy through and out and to achieve even flow.

It felt like a miracle to Ella. "I had had that problem for well over 30 years, I think," she told me. "I never really knew why I got into that sadness so often. And now it is gone, I feel free. My body feels different and my mind is so clear. Now I can see, I know, I feel that they DO love me."

We talked a few more times over the next days and Ella kept reporting how wonderful that experience had been and how it had changed things for her. Now she no longer needed to get upset about the little unpleasant things her friends and family did. They had lost their sting for her. Now many situations were so much easier. Now her relationship with her husband improved again.

Well, I had only just begun to learn a little about EmoTrance. You will probably not be surprised that after this experience I thought to myself "I have to learn this properly." So I went and did it. I became a trainer of EmoTrance. And it is a heart-felt mission for me to help many, many other people make their lives easier, better and happier with EmoTrance.

Unrequited Love was Affecting My Business

The client, let's call him Michael, had heard about me and EmoTrance from a friend of mine. What had allowed him to consider this at all was the fact that he did not have to tell me what his problem was.

So we met in his office one nice summer day around noon. Michael seemed fairly self-conscious and uneasy. He doubted that we could proceed without him telling me what his problem was. And he was extremely reluctant to talk about that.

So I quite simply asked him, "When you think about that problem, where do you feel that in your body? Show me with your hands."

Although Michael had never done any kind of energy work before he seemed to be quite sensitive to the flow and states of energies. He felt the movements and blockages of energy quite intensely. And he had some unusually strong reactions. So we worked quickly and intensely to alleviate the tensions for him.

We rapidly made some headway, quite to his surprise. However, progress then began to slow down considerably.

So we took a little break after about half an hour. That's when he started to tell me more about his problem—without me asking, by the way. It seems that with a lot of the pressure gone it wasn't such a big deal anymore.

So he had fallen madly in love with a woman who did not love him in return and she was in a relationship with another man. This made him suffer immensely. Often he emotionally slumped way down and even his work as an entrepreneur had started to suffer noticeably from this. That was the immediate reason he had even considered to ask for help. He saw his business in danger.

Knowing this helped me in guiding the process better and we were back on the success track until Michael stopped feeling anything. While he thought the entire matter was resolved I suspected an energy shield. Well, we did in fact find one. Very carefully and deliberately we followed the shield protocol and healed quite a few energetic injuries until the shield could be taken down completely.

After about an hour of EmoTrance, and moving enormous amounts of energy and healing numerous blockages and energetic wounds, Michael got pretty tired. Since I felt we had worked through the problem I readily agreed to end the session.

On the evening of that same day I had a chance to check how Michael was doing. He reported that he felt very good and that the day had passed unusually well for him. He said that he felt the same as he did before all that suffering had begun for him quite some weeks ago.

So this is the power of EmoTrance. But this is not finished yet!

About four months later I met Michael again, but he wasn't alone. With him was a pretty lady. They had been a couple for a few weeks then and seemed very, very happy together. My friend, who had put Michael and me in contact, told me that his business was getting a little less attention from Michael lately. But it wasn't as severe as it had been and for entirely different reasons! Very happy ones. ;)

From Fear and Resistance to Excitement in My New Job

Key team member Julie was involved in a departmental change and found herself in a new role. Having changed imposed created a lot of resentment together with resistance to the job due to a lack of interest and aptitude for the new role. Her previous job involved tangible objects, shipping boxes form one place to the other. Her new job was about the virtually invisible intangible world inside the boxes. She just could not get her head around it. It was not her thing. Add domestic stress and a long commute to a new job she didn't like and productivity was now a big problem with difficult relationships with new team members.

We looked at the aptitude for her new job. She had a really big shield to it and a strong resistance in her chest to even allowing any of this new technology world in. Step by step, working with that energy shield, we got her to be able to be complete open and handle what that new job was about. The result? Eagerness and enthusiasm and excitement about a whole new filed of learning that was now opened up to her.

We looked at her feelings towards a particular colleague, released that energy from her chest and her relationships also started to flow more easily. Resentment levels had reduced significantly and the employee was now happier and productivity was restored

Senior Manager Was Close to Breakdown

Tony was a senior manager in a communications company. He was stressed, feeling vulnerable in his job, tired, on the brink of a breakdown, which had been building up over two years. The stress had lead to psoriasis, IBS and his diabetes had got worse. The knock-on effect was that the stress was being taken back home. Tony was feeling threatened and unsupported in his job by his own manager and director. Much of this stress had built up as a dense energy in his chest. After 90 minutes of releasing that build up of energy, all the stress was gone together with all feelings of isolation and vulnerability. His confidence and energy was restored. Not only had he been restored back to being in control and at peak performance, but his psoriasis eventually cleared up and his wife was a lot happier with him coming home happy instead of grumpy.

Handling an Angry Customer

For a few years I was running a lot of workshops and training courses nationwide in EFT and EmoTrance, sometimes two or three per month with 20-plus people at each event. There was a lot of admin going on behind the scenes. However, sometimes if I scheduled a course in a more remote area, we didn't get enough people so we had to cancel the course, and redirect the few who had booked to the next event. Sometimes people had to cancel for various reasons. This impacted us especially if it was a small course, which could even mean an event made no profit at all. To minimise losses we discussed whether we should have a 'no refunds policy,'s offering credit to future courses in the case of cancellation. I was new to business, and taking advice this seemed like a good idea.

Diane had attended an EFT course and on the day booked and paid to attend the next EmoTrance workshop. In fact we ended up having to cancel that EmoTrance course due to low numbers and we promised we would let everyone know the next dates. It was a busy time, and due to administration oversight, Diane had been forgotten. She phoned up nine months later really angry and demanding a refund; angry that she had not heard from us and that she had paid in full for the course, and we had cancelled the one she planned to attend. I had a choice, to either quote policy at her, which would be presenting her with a brick wall guaranteed to escalate her anger of not being heard and likely to lead to threats of 'seeking legal advice,' or to handle it in an energetically intelligent way.

Having already developed my ability to handle anger and confrontation, I was relaxed and able to listen and absorb all she was saying. My response was: "You are absolutely right to be angry. We let you down and you are completely entitled to your refund. In your shoes I would be demanding the same. I am so sorry that you've received this treatment from us. I have no excuses—we simply forgot to follow up with you. Our fault completely, I'm really sorry."

In other words I was accepting and reading her energy, recognising her situation and giving her that recognition and appreciation, i.e. energy nutrition in return. With this her energy completely released. I felt her become more relaxed. Now we could discuss a solution. So with the same openness and honesty I continued: "I could give you a refund, but the main reason I don't want to is actually because of what you will miss by not attending this course. I really want you to come." I went on to remind her what we would be doing and how she would benefit from it. In fact she confessed, she did want to attend the course, she was just angry about how she had been treated. So we booked her on the next event and I offered her the chance to repeat the EFT course as a refresher as it was along time since she'd done it, and still hadn't submitted her exam work. She was completely happy, and so was I. After the EmoTrance course she emailed me to say how much she enjoyed it and had benefited from it and to thank me for the encouragement to stay with it.

This energy flow model is the core of successful customer relations programmes.

Energy needs to flow: the client's situation needs to be accepted completely and understood.

Everyone needs energy nutrition. I gave her the apology she needed and the recognition and appreciation of her situation and how she was feeling and a an extra bonus, which was icing on the cake for her.

The result? Conflict diffused and solution now possible.

After the Affair

Peter came to see me about his relationship problems. He'd had an affair a couple of years ago, but it didn't work out and he decided he wanted his wife and family. The after-effects of the affair had caused him a lot of stress. He had deep regrets and a lot of guilt. The whole episode had impacted his work and damaged his career, which he also regretted. His relationship with his wife was still strained. They lived together, but there was little or no actual connection. Peter had been down for a long time, but somehow wanted to improve his relationship if that was possible.

The plan from my side was to release all his emotional energy of guilt, to release his regrets about the impact on his marriage, and regrets about the impact on his career. Then he felt more relaxed and was ready to restore his relationship with his wife. Knowing that his wife wasn't ready, so him seeking attention and appreciation from her would not be received well yet, we focussed on helping Peter to feel greater love for himself, in order that he didn't need to seek that affirmation in Jackie.

So we did some affirmations about feeling good. I made him say "I'm a great father," "I love myself," "I'm stunningly attractive to the opposite sex." Each of these affirmations triggered all kinds of resistances within, such as, "I'm not so great a father, I'm a bit too strict sometimes," so we softened and flowed until he felt it was 100 percent true.

When working on, "I love myself" there was resistance: "But its weird to say that about yourself, especially as a guy," and "Won't I become big headed if I love myself more?" and "In the services we're programmed not to recognise our own feelings, so it feels weird to say this." We softened and flowed releasing all these energy disturbances and by the time he could accept "I'm a stunning guy and women love me," his own self esteem and self love was at an all time high. He felt terrific, and left on a high, feeling so fulfilled in himself he didn't need to seek anything from Jackie, especially while she still needed lots of space and time.

Not knowing how things would work out in the long run between them, we also discussed how he might feel about the possible outcomes; if they reconciled or if they split. We cleared any negative emotions and conflicts around each scenario, and even released his fears about other unfulfilled dreams he had, that he might be able to pursue them if they decided to separate. At the end he had the clarity and relaxed acceptance to be able to handle whichever way the relationship might go.

I asked if Jackie might now come to see me. Jackie and I had a few sessions too. There was a lot of hurt and anger and resentment about various episodes in the past, which we released by softening and flowing. There was also stress to release about other events in her life where she felt unsupported, e.g. when her grandmother died. It also came to be apparent that they had married very young when she had fallen pregnant, and the path to motherhood at the expense of her career was a big issue for her. We softened and flowed it all. My aim was only to create the clarity for her to work out what she wanted with her husband, without all the past emotions getting in the way.

In the end they decided to go their separate ways. But the decision was not from resentment, hurt and anger, carrying old wounds on into the next relationship, but from healing and from clarity about what they both wanted and what was right for them.

Audition Nerves: from Panic to Passion

Jannine, once my Admin Manager, was also a part-time cabaret artist. She loved singing and performing and had entered South Coast Idol singing contest. Jannine tells her story...

"After four hours of queuing to audition among 300 hopefuls I got through the first round to the top 35 who were called back for a second audition. We all had to sit in a room together and we were all nervous. My audition was second to last, which made it even worse because I was seeing everyone else coming out saying how bad it was. About 15 minutes before my audition my nerves started to turn into panic and I was almost shaking. This was my one chance to show what I could do and I didn't want to mess it up. So I phoned my boss, Sandra Hillawi, for some EmoTrance on the phone! All concerns about what anyone else would be thinking as we did this by phone went out the window, as this was so important for me.

Sandra asked me, "Where do you feel all the panic in your body?" It was really, really, hot in my chest. She told me to focus on the energy in my chest and think of it softening. It wouldn't soften! I was feeling even more panicky now. Then she asked me to tap on the karate chop point on the side of my hand saying, "Even though I'm feeling all this panic and it's not softening I love and accept myself." Suddenly it all started to flow upwards into my throat. The heat shifted into my throat, through my cheek and.... out through my ear.... how weird is that?! My friend said she could see my skin going red moving up my chest to my throat and into my cheeks. When all the energy had left I felt brilliant and my confidence was a 9/10. I was ready to go, but that wasn't good enough for Sandra. We did some more EmoTrance until I was totally confident. I went in and I sang One Day in Your Life by Anastacia and I admit I was fantastic and I loved it. One of the judges even clapped. The voice coach and second judge said I really stood out because I was the only one who didn't have any nerves and was able to be herself. My boss, Sandra, got a box of chocs and a bunch of flowers as I'm now off to a recording studio to make the singing clip that the general public gets to vote on at South Coast Idol's website, which makes up part of the score in the grand final!"

Ecstasy and Oneness on the Subway

I recently attended the first EmoTrance training here in the U.S. Through a series of unexpected events I found myself staying at a hotel in New Jersey, even though the training was held in Queens, New York. So I had to take a bus and subway ride (on the 'E' train) every morning to get to the training.

On the second day of the training I was riding in, surrounded by people, lost in my own thoughts. At one point I closed my eyes, went inside myself, and noticed both how LOUD the subway was (New York trains are frightfully loud, they CLANG! they SCREEEEECH! they sway TO AND FRO, they make nasty grating metal-on-metal sounds, etc), and that I had 'shut down' to 'protect' myself against this awful intrusion into my psyche. I then realized that I had shut down and was resisting it, and so I decided to see whether I could open up to it, and 'soften and flow.' I began doing that, and after some initial fear and resistance, I experienced this powerful and incredibly delicious sense of ecstasy, as I allowed all the sounds, clangs, bangs and screeches to just flow through me, and I felt the JOY/THRILL/ECSTASY of experiencing myself as part (rather than separate) of several thousand of tons of steel hurtling through space at 80 miles/hour. It totally changed my experience of riding on the subway, both in that moment and afterwards as well.

From Pain Release to a Happier Life

Let me first tell you how I came to know Sandra. What a fabulous human being! I am an explorer by nature; by default; by make-up. I am a voracious curious soul incarnated in a mind. I was Googling this day about other Energy methods related to EFT. You know, sometimes it is like shopping for a particular thing, and you wind up buying some other valuable diamond. So I was shopping for an alternative and came across the EmoTrance website, and then came across Sandra's name and website. Of course, I emailed her immediately for nothing more than just probing. I emailed her and then almost immediately received an answer. She asked me to add her to my Skype. I felt like a rooster. Who would receive an invitation for a chat with one of the pioneers of EmoTrance and wouldn't feel like a rooster. But actually I felt like a humbled rooster.

At that time I was recuperating from surgery in a very sensitive area with tremendous pain. And this was about three days after the operation. Sandra offered to work on the pain of the operation and I accepted. She worked with me on the pain for almost 15 minutes, and as she worked with me, the pain really decreased. She asked me to do the simple proviso of EmoTrance which is to 'soften and flow.' I softened and flowed, and all of sudden I was taken by surprise when the pain started to decrease geometrically. And in a matter of 15 minutes, the pain was almost gone except for a minimal trace and my inflated ego was gone too, leaving behind it a humbled person who really experienced a new territory in his own soul and an easy path to spirituality.

I tried EmoTrance on my own two days later and was able to let go of this pain completely. I made two discoveries about EmoTrance from this experience. First: The simpler the way the things are, the more effective they are. Second: I needed some time to get 'in tune' with this new healing method to move to the next level. Since then, I can't count how many times I find myself during every day of life now reminding myself that every thing is just energy and asking the energy stuck in my body to flow and go. Happiness and joy was within me, not outside me, and this simple technique has been a way of discovering more about myself and about life.

From Shame to Love

I'd been gaining weight again. The last few years I'd been struggling with my weight; it increased then I'd go on a diet to reduce. The Cambridge diet worked well for me and I lost the weight, but it didn't address my eating issues—it just put them aside. So when I started eating again, nothing had changed, the old habits kicked in again so I regained the weight. My weight had reached its maximum even and I didn't like my body anymore. But still I was overeating.

My interest and compassion for human suffering in the world was growing and I was also feeling a hypocrite. Here was I claiming to care yet when so many didn't even have one meal a day, here I was part of the over-indulgent Western culture, eating to excess, indulging on biscuits, and extravagantly leaving the lights and heating on in my house… while other nations were paying the price of my greed and extravagance, being plundered for their resources to fuel my extravagant lifestyle. I was reading, informing myself, claiming to care, and now I was feeling ashamed. But I couldn't stop my behaviour; it was an automatic programme, which had been running for a long time. In fact all of this was below the surface. What was present on the surface was listlessness and inertia. I had no motivation for work and felt disconnected from it—and I was feeling needy in terms of emotional support.

I booked a session with my ET buddy, to focus on getting motivated for work again. As I started to get the energy flowing and what came up was that I didn't feel like I loved myself right now. It felt like a 6/10. The lack of love feelings were in my chest and in my head. We worked through releasing this until I could love myself about 9/10, but I just couldn't get to the last bit. Silent tears were streaming down my face. That was my shame about my eating habits, partly about my size, partly that this has been going on so long, but mostly about my hypocrisy. As we focussed on this energy in my chest I felt a wave moving down my body to my legs and a dawning of lightness, like a new me was emerging, a more compassionate me. I felt it was becoming possible to love myself, while not disrespecting and being blind to others who are less fortunate at the same time. A way to becoming a more moderate person was emerging. It was scary, as without my old self-indulgent habits that helped me so much in the past, who would I be? How would I cope? This energy was still in my chest and my head. Tears were still streaming. We continued to focus on these energies, breathing through them until the waves flowing downwards subsided. The whole session lasted an hour. I felt a bit washed out afterwards, but I felt different. A real change had occurred.

That evening I didn't have the appetite for a meal, I had two apples instead. The next morning again it felt different. I was conscious of my eating and the large appetite was gone. I didn't feel like I wanted a lot. I had a small bowl of porridge made with water and a little honey. That was more than enough to satisfy me. Before, I would have had a larger bowl made with milk, raisins and honey on top. I felt a more moderate person now. I felt centred and in control. I felt thankful and humble to be in a land where I can make myself a breakfast, when so many others do not have the same privilege. I think of them and offer a prayer for them while I eat. I pray also that in my circumstances of good fortune that I may use that sustenance and good fortune well in the service of others.

It feels like a new era has dawned for me and really I feel like I have shed an old skin at last. My energy for work is back and I love myself again. I accept my body even though it's larger than it's ever been. But that's the result of the old me, doing the best that she could. I don't feel the need to diet. I accept and love my body as it is. I feel that continued moderation and the new compassionate consciousness in my eating and my lifestyle, the fact that my needs are a fraction of what they were, will allow some balance to be restored in time and in a gentle and more natural way. That the energy body has released that which it has been holding onto for so long, and that now it's gone, the physical body can follow. And it is.

Transforming Emotional Energy as a Way of Life

EmoTrance is a way of living: a generous way of living with energy and with this whole beautiful universe. The other day I was down and hurt in a seemingly promising romantic relationship, and I was supposed to receive a phone call, but this phone call never came through. I was down; I tried to call her but no avail. The phone kept ringing on the other side, but there was no response. I felt betrayed... I felt annoyed... I felt cheap... I felt that there must be something inside me that renders me unsuccessful to a large extent in my own relationships. And you can add whatever you would like to add of mean qualities I felt about myself in this day..Oh boy—it was a day!

The next day I saw Sandra online. Sandra is ready to uplift you if you are overseas or underseas or in any other place in the universe...and this speaks volumes about her unwavering faith in EmoTrance... This faith seldom escapes any person who comes across EmoTrance or across Sandra...Sandra: Cindrella of EmoTrance.

Anyway, I was wary of sharing this situation with anybody, but the intelligence of Sandra kicked in. She immediately asked me, "What's wrong with you?" I answered diplomatically that I was exhausted and had many personal issues to deal with... and then she started the wonderful dance of EmoTrance with me.

It went to a very great extent like this:

Sandra: "Where is this feeling of 'having to deal with your personal issues'?"

Me: "I feel it as heaviness in my chest and neck."

Sandra: "Can you 'soften and flow'?"

Me: "Yeah. Give me some time please. I can see the energy moving down to my navel."

Sandra: "What consistency would you give this energy?"

Me: "It seems as if it is ice that is stuck in my navel. Please give me some time to let this energy flow."

Sandra: "You can 'fast forward' the flow of the energy by imagining the addition of hot water to the ice."

Me: "Sandra, it works! Ooh, I feel like I'm a bird who's flying, but still feel some heaviness in my foot… more softening… ah, now that's gone too."

Sandra: "What is it you are looking for; what is it you really want?"

Me: "Love and happiness—someone to love and care about me."

Sandra: "When you think about love, happiness and the person who will care about you, where do you feel that?"

Me: "It is right out there before me to the left side."

Sandra: "Can you bring this energy into your body and feel it?"

I softened and flowed the energy and really I discovered there are many issues and things that I never touched on before. For example, while I was letting the energy soften and flow, I felt that there was a hand that was actually pressing on my neck and impairing me from fully enjoying my natural breath… also there was a great wound in my heart area that needed to soften and heal.

As the energy was flowing through and leaving my body, there were some remaining bits stuck, so I still had to work on in my navel to totally let the buried energy flow. As I was releasing all this energy certain memories were coming into my mind, which were behind these feelings of hurt and feeling bad about myself. I also found that however complex all these buried emotional issues were, we just focussed on the energy softening and releasing. EmoTrance made it so simple and I didn't have to disclose anything of these past memories to Sandra. I found it so interesting that EmoTrance let me unveil and release things, which at a deep unconscious level were affecting my daily life now.

I emerged from this cleansing process feeling totally great and much more capable of seeing my self-worth and self-esteem despite whatever may be going on around me. This session taught me some valuable lessons. I always learn a lot when I've transformed the energy of whatever problem I have. This way I find that EmoTrance in my life really is a great teacher. This time I learned that:

1. It's better to deal with things sooner rather than later as putting off dealing with these issues—like heart issues—we are just prolonging the agony or 'sucking moments' in life.

2. Taking the time to digest and integrate EmoTrance in my life was like having a diamond. The more I used it the cleaner, more polished and more valuable it became to me. EmoTrance is fun and has helped me have the most wonderful experiences in life.

3. The third important thing I learned was to stop reading book after book about how I can better myself and to actually start practising it! I feel that I now have all the resources I need. Personally I am dedicating a week to each exercise in this book, doing it over and over again with different scenarios and for each of the challenges I face in my life. In short, I now know that I am always my own master and liberator.

Yes, I Can Fall in Love, as Often as I Want!

I've had a really bad time over the years with romantic relationships, always falling in love with the wrong people who didn't love me in return. The last of these one-sided affairs was so long and so painful, I really must have made some terrible decisions in the darkest hours; the result was that I kept totally away from any person or place or event where I could be tempted to fall in love again.

Two years after I discovered EmoTrance, and having done a lot of energy work on various issues (although never on that last love disaster!), I saw this man at training and…Oh dear: The golden lights; the angel choir! Oh NO! And of course, he's married, and of course, he doesn't feel the same way about me…same old story…

But this time, I had EmoTrance.

This time, and EVERY TIME, I started to feel longing or wanting I just went straight into action with it and didn't stop until it was all gone and clear. But I didn't stop with the negatives. Every time I felt love or hope or was about to go off into lala land with illusions or dreams about the future, I did the same thing. It's only energy, right?

It was amazing and exquisite, how different I felt this time around. The whole 'lovesick puppy' business never really got off the ground. I felt strong, energized, powerful and congruent. Within a week, the incidents of emotional waves of one kind or the other were reduced to a few here and there, and they were just little niggles. Ten days and it was all gone.

Ten days. The last time this had happened to me, it had taken FIFTEEN YEARS OF AGONY to survive it—and only just, and not intact by any means.

This time, with the help of EmoTrance, I was in control. And there was no sense of loss or misery or anything else—just a wonderful energized clarity, and eventually, THE realisation that:

↵ I can fall in love as often as I want to!

↜ It doesn't matter anymore if 'he' doesn't love me back.

↜ It's not about 'him,' whoever he may be. It's about me. I want to love, I can love, and finally I can love without killing myself in the process.

↜ I don't have to be afraid of love anymore.

That's priceless, wonderful—and the only thing left now is a feeling of deep sorrow that I didn't know that earlier; that I didn't know how to do that—how to work with these huge waves of emotions and ride them like a surfer, leaving me safely on the shore and sparkling, clean and clear, and bright awake.

And where do I feel this sorrow in my body?

Excuse me for a moment…there is something I need to take care of…

EmoTrance in My Life

After my weekend of EmoTrance I felt so full of love (and still do) that nothing was going to faze me.

In particular my husband is going to China on Sunday. Normally I would have moaned for so many reasons:

1. He is going on a Sunday.

2. He is going away again…

3. It's to China—what a fabulous experience (but not taking me).

4. I'm being dumped on with kids, work, etc, and so on and so on…

I have worked on all these issues softening and flowing and genuinely don't feel them any more. I really am excited for him that he is having this opportunity—he can't quite get his head around the transformation. :-)

I have had some challenges to my new model this week and have EmoTranced every one of them. I have also had some wonderful experiences. Today I witnessed a Hindu Blessing for my neighbour who is getting married tomorrow. I sat there as the Priest chanted and invited many gods to be present and let in, softened and flowed all that love, joy, and happiness, every Ohm expressed and it felt amazing, tingly, enriching and wonderful. What a fantastic way to live.

I have used it on a client for a particular issue before I went on to do a traditional healing. I have also asked to see blockages by proxy during healing. A client this week said she thought the healing felt very different from ever before (she has been coming for healing for three years).

So thank you from my heart. Learning about EmoTrance has been life enhancing, life changing and enriching.

Married 20 Years and Never Knew What Love Was

I was talking to a friend, who has been married for 20 years with 3 children. He was having some problems in his relationship. He was a really nice guy with a great heart. He worked hard and as a result was away from his family a lot.

I asked him, "If I was to say to you, did you get the shopping today and did you remember to buy the new clothes for the kids? How would you feel?"

He replied: "I don't feel anything—this is normal everyday life."

Then I asked: "If I said to you that you are a really good man with a heart of gold and I really appreciate how hard you work for your family, how would you feel now?"

He smiled, "Wow, I feel all nice and warm inside."

I introduced him to the concept of emotional food, explaining that he was feeling good from my recognition and appreciation, from my heart to his heart. I explained that he was giving his wife and family the physical food and attending to their physical needs admirably, but when did he last give them emotional food? They needed this just as much as the food on their table.

I asked him for the next two weeks to find something every day to say to his wife, that was genuine and from the heart; to recognise something about her and tell her. "That's it, that's all you have to do; recognise and appreciate something every day to your partner," I said, and gave him an analogy:

It's like you have this flower at home that's wilting and closed. And you have the sun in your heart. Sure, you make sure she gets fed, food and water on the table, but she gets no sunshine from you, yet you have so much sun inside you. You expect her to blossom and you complain there is no perfume when she gets no sun. Pay more attention to her. Direct some of your heart energy to your wife; give her some genuine recognition and appreciation, and just watch her open up and blossom.

Then you take can pleasure and enjoy that beauty and fragrance that comes back to you. Do this and I can guarantee that you will have a different relationship at the end of two weeks. When I spoke to him again, as predicted, they were much closer and much happier.

He had never really had the know-how or understanding about that. Twenty years into his relationship, he said that love was something on the television and in romantic songs. It wasn't a real experience that he felt in his life, but love was starting to grow for him now after 20 years. Finally, now his wife was so much happier and started to feel appreciated, recognised she was giving attention back to him from that happy state and he started to get the nourishment back in return. The circle of energy flow and acceptance, and energy nutrition was now working.

Healing Aisha

Aisha actually came to me for a detox. She had a number of physical symptoms, daily headaches, monthly migraines, constipation and extremely heavy periods. She was also very tense, described herself as impatient and angry and had a history of a lot of stress. She could date her headaches back to when she was 13 years old. She was now 35. I took her through the cleanse programme, but while we had our time together we worked on releasing some of her stress starting with the headaches.

At work there were certain situations that made her angry; certain behaviours from people she worked with. I asked her to think of these events one by one, and to locate where the pressure was in her body. Most of it was in her head. We softened and flowed. We reached a point in a few minutes where she was surprised and amazed that now the same behaviours she really didn't mind at all, and laughed about it. Between this session and the next she had no headaches until the day of our next appointment. This work took about 20 minutes.

I tested her on what we had done the last time; how she was handling certain situations at work. All of them were fine now. There were a few situations at home with her husband that she had difficulty with, like when he said "hmmmph" and looked at her in a knowing judging way, which really used to make her angry. She would normally shout at him in response. One by one I directed her to think about all behaviours that were a problem and we released the energy sometimes from her stomach flowing down and out, sometimes from her head.

Then I turned to her past migraines. I asked if she could recall what was actually going on when she had her first migraine. She remembered it well, and it was no surprise to find the pressure was back in her head. We softened and flowed. A lot of energy released through her ears. I asked how many really memorable migraines she'd had, and could she recall what was going on then? There were another four really distressing events. We located the energy stored for each event, mostly in the head and released it in the same way.

We had some time to spare so while we were at it, I was asked if there was anything else we could do. For example, if she were to run through her life and recall any other stressful events, we had time to release some of them. There was one in particular that was very intense. The energy was again in her head, but also in her forehead. She said she was feeling really angry when she recalled it. Again, we released all this energy and continued for all other stressful events she could recall.

So far, I had no knowledge whatsoever of her past. All I did was ask if there was a particular memory and have her think about it and locate the energy in the body. Then I tested by asking her to recall the memory again and any new details that came to her that were still a problem. She released everything completely without having to reveal a single detail to me.

At the end of the session, about 40 minutes this time, she said she really didn't feel angry at all now. She felt totally in control; so much lighter and so much more relaxed. She is now free of her headaches completely and her tolerance and ability to handle difficult behaviours and situations at work vastly improved. Her husband was delighted with his new relaxed, happy and healthier wife!

Losing Weight with EmoTrance
Contributed by an ET Practitioner.

I have been using EmoTrance on a course I have developed to help people lose weight and feel better about themselves by understanding the root causes of overeating, such as habitual eating, comfort eating, sabotage and low self esteem. It soon became apparent when working with clients that low self esteem was a key factor because when you feel bad about yourself and your body you tend to not care what you eat; not caring about feeding yourself with nutritious food, but opting for high fat or high sugar foods instead—and not have any respect for the wonderful machine that is the human body.

I have used EmoTrance with great success dissolving blockages about past hurtful comments and remarks that are being held in the energy system with regard to a person's shape, weight or personality. All these 'digs'—sometimes stemming from childhood, such as puppy fat and remarks about being on another diet or liking puddings, etc., get stored in the energy system and further undermine a person's confidence. The client in question had several hurtful remarks made to her and I took each one in turn asking her to think about the situation where she received the hurtful comment. She could immediately feel the painful, tight uncomfortable feelings as though I had just made the comment directly to her. The memory was as vivid as the day it was first said. Gently guiding the client with my own intention I helped her to focus on the blocked energy, which in this case was over her heart and stomach area, and allowed it to soften and flow out of the body. The energy moved with quite some speed and grace up and out of her ears. It was almost as though her ears had heard the remark and had kept that energy inside her. We revisited the memory and found that she had no emotional attachment to the remark and seemed unconcerned and indifferent about what the person had thought and said to her at that time. We did the same with several other hurtful comments and each time the hurt was being stored in the same area. It seemed little surprise that the client's main weight carrying area was around her stomach, directly where the comments were being stored.

I also used the technique to help her deal with criticisms that she was ingesting into her energy field and helped her to receive compliments that she was shielding. A heartfelt compliment had made the client cross her arms, giggle and feel very self conscious. Through loving guidance I was able to show her how wonderful you can feel when the beautiful words travel through your energy and give you a tingly feeling and warm sensation. Self esteem is just one aspect of weight issues, but it is a very big aspect and the client is feeling so much more confident in her own skin. She has no emotional attachment to her past in relation to her weight and is making huge strides forward to becoming a slimmer, confident, vibrant person who no longer requires eating for comfort and to fill an emotional void through food.

I Love Her and I Hate Her

Hugh had been with Mags for some time, but they had separated. Hugh adored Mags, but Mags had experienced some painful childhood traumas and certain situations would trigger sudden intense anger and very aggressive behaviour. Hugh works in personal development and had tried hard to adapt and be able to handle this, and he had also had tried to help Mags, but she was not willing or able to 'go there' to do her own healing—until now. Hugh had to leave the relationship as he just couldn't handle her anger, her spitefulness and her volatility.

The situation was complicated as Mags had recently fallen pregnant and Hugh was in a dilemma: to stay and work things out with Mags, as without these outbursts she was his ideal woman—or to accept he just couldn't hack it and seek a new relationship.

He had already met someone really nice, but the spark wasn't there with her—not like it was with Mags. But he couldn't shake Mags off and really didn't know what to do.

Hugh came to me to see if we could help him find a way forward.

We started to focus on how he felt when he tried to help her and she refused to accept his help. He said this made him feel worthless, and felt a great heaviness in his chest. While we were focussing to release this a memory came to him about his aunt. At one time his aunt had really laid into him about something she thought Hugh had done, which she had misunderstood. Her verbal bullying was difficult to accept and her particular comments that he was not a good person ever since he was two years old, made him feel worthless, taking away the only thing he had: his goodness of character. We cleared this energy from this past memory, and again a new insight arose that he despised unjust bullying. He was experiencing all-over body anger as he connected with this insight. We softened and flowed and released it. He recognised a connection between behaviour in his aunt and behaviour in Mags. He thought that was interesting that, Mags was triggering an unresolved issue for him from a past memory.

He also had an insight, which was to Hugh the crux of the whole thing. That Mags, by not accepting his help, the thing he was so good at, made him feel a failure—again, taking away his self-worth. This hurt of failing to help someone with all the tools he had, was in his chest. We released it all.

There was one remaining part to release: handling Mag's spitefulness. Again we identified where this energy was and released it.

We reflected on the fact that life had sent him this relationship to show up some areas he needed to heal within himself. And that also Mags may not be able to or willing to ever completely release her old traumas and that maybe he might not be the person to facilitate that, and that maybe rather than trying to change her he might develop the capacity to accept her and love her as she is.

I asked him about the bullying and how did he feel now. He said that before, if he saw someone being bullied, he would want to intervene to protect the victim, but his reaction would have been angry. Now he said he would still want to intervene, but he could also see the person who was being aggressive and be able to engage with them and recognise that they also have a problem.

After all of that Hugh felt a new clarity and a real change within. He now felt he could be supportive towards Mags as well as more accepting. He saw what he had previously thought was only a problem in Mags, also triggered a problem within himself, which he had now healed, and by healing his compassion had grown.

Which path he chooses—time will only tell, but Hugh's final words to me were: "Whatever happens, now there will be less stress between us. That's not only good for us, but its going to be good for our baby."

Loving My Second Child was Harder Than the First

When Karla had her second child there were some complications at birth and her new baby son had to spend two weeks in an incubator at the hospital, while she returned home. She visited each day, but even when baby Jason came home, she didn't bond with him as much as she had bonded with her first child. Jason, now four years old, had lung problems, tended to get infections and coughed a lot. This was his normal state of health.

We started with Karla. This was straightforward to clear. We focused on the trauma and stress of the birth and the days afterwards; we released the energy of the stress. She said she also felt great guilt and sadness about leaving him each day. We located that energy in the stomach and the heart, softened and released it. I asked how strong her love was for him now and she was overjoyed to feel it as strongly as her connection with her first child.

I suggested that we might try to do something for little Jason. His first two weeks of life must have been quite traumatic for him too, leaving energy disturbances within his own system. I suggested that we might try to connect with those energies and see if we could release them for him.

I asked her to think about Jason in the incubator and to tune into what feelings he might have been having at that time in the strange environment. Then I asked where she felt it in her body. She felt his fear in her chest, so we softened and released it. She then felt his abandonment in her lungs. We softened and released that energy. She felt his aloneness and lack of maternal connection—again, in her chest area. We softened and released that. We continued until we could identify no more emotions that Jason might have experienced during that two-week period.

When I saw Karla for our next session, she was overjoyed. Not only was her relationship so much better with Jason, but his coughing had decreased significantly and his breathing was so much better.

Drinking in His Love Dissolved All My Stress

I remember one day I'd become worked up about financial issues. The undercurrents of worry were building and I found myself with a pressure headache and feeling nauseous. All I could do was go to bed in the dark and try to sleep it off. I didn't usually get headaches, so I knew the stress was getting to me.

I had a call from my husband while I was in bed. I talked little, just listened. I heard the care and love in his voice, as he reassured me, his words coming from the heart. Knowing how to really absorb that energy I drank it in. I just drank and drank and drank, listening to him and letting all that love and care flow through me. I went to sleep peacefully and the next morning I felt totally amazing. I was crystal clear in everything. No stress, a clear head, loads of energy and joy. Every little thing that had been building up all week that culminated in the previous night's ordeal had vanished completely. Wow, the energy of his love had flowed through me and dissolved and released all the different energy disturbances I had.

I was in awe and rejoiced at the healing power of love.

Love Healed and Transformed Us Both

This is a very personal story and some of the details I will omit out of respect for others involved. Something happened that completely turned our loving, trusting relationship upside down and inside out. I came to learn something about my fiancé that was such a total shock, I was stunned. It was so out of character that it destroyed my whole belief system. I didn't know who he was anymore. The trust was gone completely. I was devastated. He had lied to me and I had trusted him totally. Apparently it had been going on for some time. He was also devastated at the disaster arriving in our relationship. He could hardly walk. His leg was numb and had no strength. He'd had problems with his leg since a car accident years earlier and two months prior had had follow up surgery. He was limping and experiencing numbness in his foot due to nerve damage. But now his whole leg was numb and he could hardly stand. Such was his own distress.

This could have been the end of a beautiful relationship, but because of how we handled it, it became a moment of complete transformation and healing in him, including physical healing, and a deepening of our love and trust.

We had had a year of pure love and happiness and it was a lot to let go of. Both of us wanted our relationship, so the only way to heal was complete openness and honesty about what had been happening and why. That meant he had to tell me every single detail, however painful to him and however painful to me, and I had to listen with an open heart, to absorb and accept this, and somehow to soften, flow and let it go.

It was a painful process. It was hard to open my heart to listen but I did. He cried at all the painful details, his pain at hurting me, his pain of regret, his stupidity in thinking, he was so sorry. I absorbed it all, it hurt me, tears flowed, I softened and flowed.

Then it was my turn to speak. He had to listen to me as I expressed my feelings, my anger, my hurt, how could he do that? What kind of a man does something like that? It was his turn to accept everything from me, to be open to absorb it all. It was painful for him, but he took it all from me.

Then a miracle happened. When everything was said on each side, it was all ok again. It was done. The love was back but now a deeper love than ever before. He felt this love and acceptance and forgiveness so deeply. It flowed through his whole body; he felt it physically. It completely energised and renewed him. He stood up and walked about. His leg problem had gone. He had 90 percent strength back in his leg, and only a tiny numbness at his toes remained. We were both so amazed and overjoyed. We focused our attention on the remaining numbness in his toes, with the intention for the energy to soften and flow. It did, and it completely released. He now had 100 percent strength in his leg for the first time in years. He walked up and down the stairs putting weight on it to test it, but it was gone—100percent!

My fiancé was a new man—not only physically, but emotionally. He'd had a transformation. His energy and joy for work was at an all-time high. He woke up bright in the mornings, worked joyfully through the day, came home, slept all through the night, which is something he had not done for a long time. He even stopped smoking and was so happy. He had learned a profound lesson about the power of honesty, openness and trust. Something in his heart changed. He became a new and even better man than he was before. We rejoiced and rejoice still not only because we saved what we could have lost, but for all that we gained from the healing power and transforming power of love and the even greater love we now share.

The whole episode from the shattering news to the healing and renewal took no more than 24 hours. Incredible, but true.

What was a disaster in our relationship, when faced and handled fully with an open heart, brought us both such immense learning, happiness and love, and as such is now regarded as no less than a wonderful blessing for which we are both deeply grateful.

Overcoming Procrastination to Write This Book

19 November 2007

I am an author. I feel such joy to say that, as right now I haven't even written the book, but at the same time I feel like I've finished.

I've just come off the phone from a fab EmoTrance session with my ET buddy Baya, a fellow EmoTrance trainer and dear friend, and she has helped me get into the energy state of having finished the book.

This energy of completion is amazing. "I am an author" fills me with joy and delight! This flow of energy has made the book I am about to write flow so easily.

How did we start? Well I've been procrastinating about this for ages. It's my first book too. I had blocks about writing, structure, purpose, connecting with the readers and fears about 'who am I to write a book?'—all of which were doing a great job of maintaining the status quo of inaction.

"So Baya, I want to write the book now, can you help me with that?"

I had just come back from launching EmoTrance in New York, in November 2007. It was a fabulous event and I felt my own energy even more strongly as I was teaching—warm, passionate, open, relaxed, confident and generous. Baya asked me to connect with that. That was easy. It was flowing powerfully through me and out. Then she asked me, "Where do you feel the energy about writing?" The whole warm power flowing energy disappeared in an instant, and I felt this small tight feeling inside me. So we softened and released this energy. It flowed up and out through my head. Now writing felt very different: much more possible; much more present.

The next block was the structure for the book. When I thought about this concept, I felt a cloudy energy out front, blocking my vision and a heavy energy in my shoulders. We softened and released in my shoulders then softened the energy outside, brought it in, through and out.

Now I had a real sense of the purpose of the book, which lead me to think about readers. I was able to connect with the readers in the professional practitioners and trainers of EmoTrance and other energy therapies, such as EFT and energy healers. But what about the general public who would want to read and get benefit from this? I had no connection with them. That sense was, once again, out there somewhere, over to the left, in front of me.

Again, I softened the energy, brought it in, through and out. It was a struggle, and the areas of resistance in my body had to be softened to let it all in, through and out. But we got it all flowing. It was a soft energy, and I was starting to feel joy and love in connecting with the readers. Now to merge all the readers' energies, my professional audience, the public and….whoah—there was a fear… the gurus, the experts, the existing authors. I had a block in my chest about this, so I softened and released it. Then I was able to take in and connect with everyone. The flow was great but gentle. I thought of it speeding up and it started to flow faster and became stronger and more invigorating in my body.

So now I was connecting with and drawing strength and power from my reader audience. That felt good. Next Baya said: "I want you to think 'I've finished it, and I have my finger on the send key to send it to the publisher'." There was a moment of joy, but wow there followed a heavy block like a brick the size of my whole torso. We softened this and released it, then I started to feel fantastic, so energised, happy and joyful; the real sense of completion was streaming through my whole being. "I'm an author," I said and laughed out loud.

The final step was the content. I created the intention: "All the ideas, stories, theory, wisdom and learning required for this book are flowing to me in the right sequence." I invited them in, through and out. They flowed easily in the strong passionate flow already created. Then again: "All the content has already flowed to me; the book is finished," and as I now write I still feel the excitement of this energy.

I marvel at the power of the Law of Attraction at work. I have created the energy, the state of flow and completion for the book that is written energetically and now just needs to flow through my keyboard onto the pages. This last bit now seems so easy! And so with great joy happiness and excitement I begin.

Thank you Baya for being the best ET buddy!

P.S Four weeks later, the first draft of the book was sent to the publisher.

References

1. *The Field: The Quest for the Secret Force of the Universe* by Lynn McTaggart.

2. *Molecules of Emotion: The Science Behind Mind-Body Medicine* by Candace Pert.

3. *The Biology of Belief* by Bruce Lipton.

4. *Oceans of Energy* by Dr Silvia Hartmann.

5. *Tapping the Healer Within* by Roger Callahan.

6. Gary Craig's website for EFT: www.emofree.com.

7. Tapas Flemming's website for TAT: www.tatlife.com.

8. *EMDR and the Energy Therapies* by Dr Phil Mollon.

9. *Living Energy* by Dr Silvia Hartmann.

10. *The Secret* by Rhonda Byrne; explaining the Law of Attraction.

11. http://www.informationclearinghouse.info/article18789.htm.

12. http://www.hooponopono.org/Articles/beyond_traditional_means.html.

13. http://www.mrfire.com/article-archives/new-articles/worlds-most-unusual-therapist.html.

14. EmoTrance is based on The Harmony Programme 1993 www.a1harmony.com.

Additional Resources

1. Where to find The Love Clinic courses in your area:
   www.lovecliniconline.com or www.sandrahillawi.com

2. Book a consultation with Sandra Hillawi:
   Tel: UK +44 (0)23 92 433928 or email: sandra@lovecliniconline.com

3. Order more copies of The Love Clinic online:
   www.lovecliniconline.com

4. Order the e-book:
   www.lovecliniconline.com

5. Share your story:
   Send an email to sandra@lovecliniconline.com or submit it via the *Articles* section of the website at www.lovecliniconline.com

6. Join a TLC group and make new ET friends for mutual healing, support and personal development:
   www.lovecliniconline.com

7. Find an EmoTrance Practitioner near you:
   www.emotrance.com

8. Learn about Energy Dancing, releasing energetic injuries and healing to music:
   www.lovecliniconline.com

Other Useful Links

1. www.emotrance.com: The official EmoTrance website with more reading and articles about EmoTrance

Finding an EmoTrance Practitioner or Trainer

The following experienced Practitioner/Trainers contributed client stories to this book:

Kim Bradley: ET Trainer, UK, 44 (0)7970 584 851
Kim@heavens-touch.co.uk

Janet Dedman: ET Trainer, UK, +44 (0)1453 542 272
janet_dedman@hotmail.com

Baya Salmon Hawk: ET Trainer, UK, 44 (0)1462 437350
hawkeye5000@gmail.com

John Freedom: ET Trainer, USA, +1-520-241-5124
freejjii@yahoo.com

Detlev Tesch: ET Trainer, Germany, +49 228 4737-92
dt@webtesch.de

Margarita Foley: ET Trainer, UK, +44 208 8019 883
Margarita@marieaux.org

Silvia Hartmann: ET Creator, UK, +44 (0)1323 729666
www.silviahartmann.com

Worldwide practitioner and trainer directory can be found at
www.emotrance.com

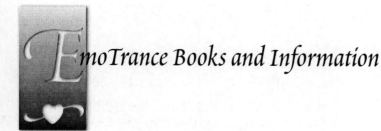

EmoTrance Books and Information

The Introduction Guide to EmoTrance
Contributors

DragonRising in co-ordination with the custodians of EmoTrance, The Sidereus Foundation, have teamed up to produce the EmoTrance 2008 yearbook. This is your perfect introduction guide to this incredible 21st century healing and self-improvement energy technique. This Paperback is densely packed with information, articles, and includes international practitioner & trainer listings.

£9.97 Paperback, Ebook £Free

Oceans of Energy: The Patterns & Techniques of EmoTrance, Vol 1
S. Hartmann

EmoTrance is a new system for handling the human energy body and thus, radically transforming human emotions and allowing the user to experience new states of bliss, peace and enchantment. This best selling manual provides a thorough grounding in the underlying principles of EmoTrance for self help and healing. It contains all the basic techniques so that the reader can get started with EmoTrance right away. Highly acclaimed, international best seller, outstanding value.

£24.95 Softback Manual, Ebook £19.95

The Enchanted World
S. Hartmann

UK researcher Dr Silvia Hartmann, creator of Project Sanctuary, The Harmony Program and EmoTrance has written this book especially as an introduction to the presuppositions of her life's work. 65 Super Concise Chapters to lay down the stepping stones for anyone to enter "The Enchanted World"—the one true Universe that sings and dances with life, and love of life. Easy to read, multilevel depth of information that speaks to the reader in a very personal fashion. Highly Recommended.

£9.95 Lighthouse Paperback, Ebook £4.95

EmoTrance BeautyT
S.Hartmann

Follow with this fascinating journey as Dr Hartmann builds a different body image from the ground up, step by step as this extraordinary training unfolds. A unique and profound healing of the oldest wounds of all, and a priceless gift to practitioners and clients with the power to change lives and destinies in a single session. This book contains a full transcript and all the original exercises and lectures from the Beauty T training.

£16.95 Paperback, Ebook £12.95

Practitioner Of EmoTrance: Online Distance Learning E-Course

Become a fully certified practitioner of EmoTrance with this superb and exciting online distance learning course.

Full to the brim with delightful information and with wonderful, challenging and immensely rewarding exercises especially designed for the distance learning student by Dr Silvia Hartmann, Creator of EmoTrance, this course will not just bring new ideas, skills, knowledge, techniques and abilities, but also the confidence to work with others and help them feel joy when there was only pain and suffering.

A fantastic online course in 8 Units, leading to full certification as a Practitioner Of EmoTrance, with experienced tutor support throughout that will transform the beginner and supercharge the experienced energy worker.

Great value, highly recommended.

Please note that this is an E-Course. All manuals, documents and course units with the exception of the official certificate are delivered in PDF format. Product images are for illustration only.

£197.00
> Includes review e-books of The Enchanted World, Oceans Of Energy, The EmoTrance Healing Circle instruction manual, 8 Unique Course Units, Tutor Support, Certification Fee (The Sidereus Foundation) & 1-Year's Practitioner License.

£97.00
> Interest Only Option. All course materials in electronic PDF format, no tutor support, no certification. Upgradable to full certification training.

Contact DragonRising

Stay in touch with DragonRising by registering on our site
www.DragonRising.com and gain access to all our free downloads.

Address

DragonRising Publishing
The StarFields Network Ltd
Compass House, 45 Gildredge Road
Eastbourne, East Sussex, BN21 4RY
United Kingdom

Phone

01323 729 666 (United Kingdom)
646 496 9857 (US + Canada)
0044 1323 729 666 (International)

Website

www.DragonRising.com

Contact Us Online:
www.DragonRising.com/contact/